Cycling
in
The Lake District

John Wood

Published by Sigma Leisure – an imprint of
Sigma Press, 1 South Oak Lane, Wilmslow, Cheshire SK9 6AR, England.

British Library Cataloguing in Publication Data
A CIP record for this book is available from the British Library.

ISBN: 1-85058-392-7

Typesetting and Design by: Sigma Press, Wilmslow, Cheshire.

Cover picture: Lingmoor Fell with the Langdale Pikes in the background (*W.S. Stainton*)

Printed by: Manchester Free Press

PREFACE

Thousands of people visit the Lake District every year. Statistics show that the vast majority of them are car touring: they drive to a beauty spot, stretch their legs, take a photograph, then drive on to a café. There are also the serious fellwalkers, who flock to scale the famous heights, and mountain bikers, increasing in number every year, thanks to a wealth of suitable fellside tracks and bridleways. On the whole though, the area is neglected by the ordinary cyclist. Perhaps not altogether surprising as much of the district is mountainous and unsuitable for leisure cycling, but there are many square miles of unspoilt countryside between the fells that are ideal for cycling, as this book attempts to show.

There were times during the research for this book, when my wheels ground to a halt and I'd have to resort to pushing my bike up seriously steep hills. I started to wonder whether this was such a practical idea for a cycling book after all. But, most of the steep climbs only took a matter of minutes and they were surprisingly few and far between, considering the nature of the landscape. Most of the roads rise and fall fairly constantly, though not severely. Besides, for every uphill struggle there is a rewarding downhill run, and the views from the tops of the hills make the exertion worthwhile.

I have tried to keep the use of A-roads to a minimum and have only used them when there is no alternative. For example, the western shore of Ullswater should not be missed, but there is only the main road, and it is busy, but unavoidable.

The routes vary considerably in length. Some are relatively easy, demanding just an hour or two. Others are longer, requiring a half, or full day. They are intended more than anything as cycle tours: routes around which to ride at your own pace, taking in some of the district's most spectacular scenery. Information is included on picnic sites, view-points, stately homes, museums and other places of interest, and – more importantly – the wayside inns and tearooms. Most of the routes can easily be joined to others in that area, so the length of your tour can be tailored to suit the time you have available.

The rides are aimed both at motorists with their cycles on board, (starting from a car park whenever possible) and for those, like myself, who step off the train at Windermere with nothing but their cycle and their sandwiches. Each route has directions to the starting point from the nearest town. There are grid references so you can pinpoint the start exactly. The abbreviation 'OS', which appears frequently in the text, stands for 'Ordnance Survey' and their excellent maps are specified for each ride.

There is no better way to travel than by cycle. You can cover much greater distances than by foot and are able to really see and experience the landscape through which you are travelling. Lakeland scenery is varied, colourful and always has something to offer, regardless of the season. It is an area well worth getting to know by bike.

John Wood

Contents

The Lake District: scene setting

The Southern and Central Lakes

The North and North-Western Lakes

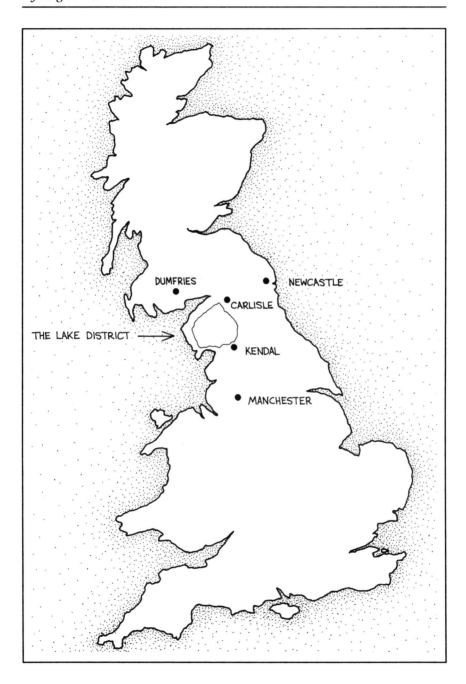

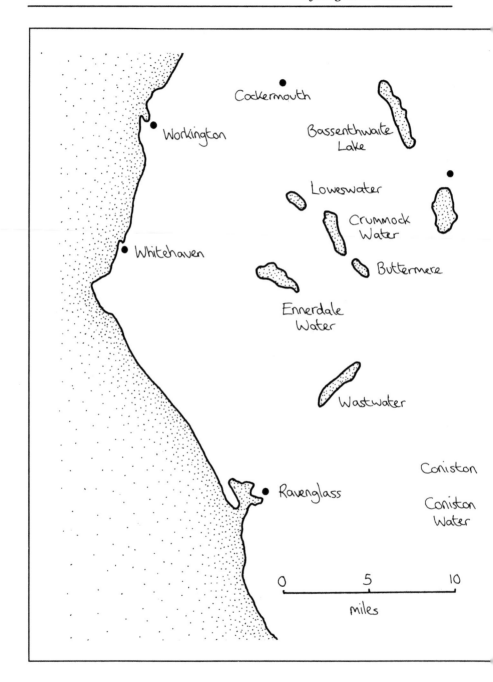

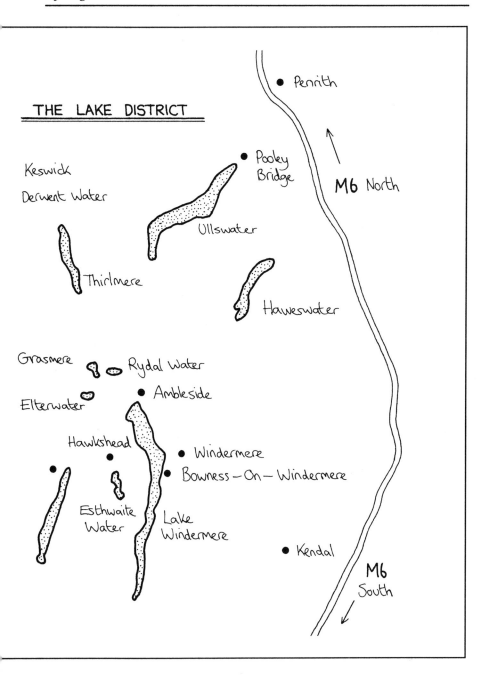

The Lake District: scene setting

Introduction

Before describing the cycle rides in this book, here is a short introduction to the geography, geology and history of the Lake District. It really is only intended as the briefest of brief introductions and there are many excellent books to read when you need more information. Some personal favourites are listed at the back of this book.

A short history . . .

The Lake District was formed when the mountains were thrown up from the Earth's crust some 450 million years ago, and is made up of some of the oldest rocks in the world. Skiddaw, for example, is older than the Alps – and they're old! There followed a period of volcanic activity and then came the Ice Ages which filled the valleys and covered most of the mountains with ice, the last one retreating only 8,000 years ago, its glaciers gouging out wide valleys (such as Great Langdale) on their way to the sea.

5,000 years ago the Lake District would have been almost completely covered with dense forests, with only the highest peaks visible above the trees. In the Neolithic (New Stone Age) period, Man, still a relative newcomer, took to chopping the trees down. He operated axe factories where 'tuffs' (particularly hard pieces of stone formed by volcanic action) were quarried and made into axe heads. One such site, very important in archaeological terms, exists in Great Langdale beneath the Langdale Pikes. The Neolithic Lakelanders were farmers and lived in wooden huts. They wore woollen clothing and made pottery food vessels.

The Bronze and Iron Ages came next, when metals were introduced and Man could fashion a blade to help with his tree cutting. He lived in villages or tribes and had the occasional battle with neighbouring settlements.

The Romans arrived in the Lakes in about 74 AD, building roads and forts such as Galava at Ambleside and Mediobogdum on the Hardnott Pass, governing the Britons for 300 years before nipping back over to Rome to sort out the Empire and all its problems.

Next, the area fell prey to Norse raiders, who eventually settled here and provided all the Scandinavian place names. In time many of them became Christians and set up home with the locals.

During medieval times, as well as farming, industry began to develop in the Lakes, such as mining on the Coniston Old Man, for example, and iron smelting on the shores of Coniston water. Vast quantities of charcoal were needed for the latter and Man again set about devastating the remaining woodlands to procure the necessary timber.

There is still a small amount of quarrying carried out in the Lakes (such as on the Kirkstone Pass) and a fair amount of farming. There is even an infamous nuclear reprocessing plant on Cumbria's western coast, but the principal industry existing today, beating the others hands down, is tourism, which provides jobs for an astounding 25,000 people.

Famous Lakelanders

The Lake District has attracted a remarkable number of talented artistic people, paticularly in literature. Here is a short selection from Words-worth to Wainwright:

William Wordsworth

Wordsworth must surely be Lakeland's most famous son. People flock from all over the world to visit his homes and his grave and to walk in his footsteps, and everyone must know at least a few lines from his 'Daffodil' poem.

He was born in 1770 in a fine house on the main street of Cocker-mouth, now owned by the National Trust, and called 'Wordsworth House'. He attended the grammar school at Hawkshead (also open to the public) where he first began to write poetry and spent most of his free time exploring the local fells.

After completing his education at Cambridge he went on a walking tour of France, quite the done thing for the single young gentleman in those days. On his travels he witnessed the French Revolution, had an affair resulting in the birth of his illegitimate daughter, then returned to England and his beloved sister, Dorothy, 21 months his junior.

In their mid-twenties, William and Dorothy spent several years living in the West Country, where they met the poet, Coleridge. The three of them spent most of their time wandering through the countryside at all hours of the day and night reciting poetry to each other, and were considered very strange by the locals, even at one point being taken for foreign spies.

'Lyrical Ballads' was a collaboration between the two poets, though William did most of the work. It was not that well received at the time, but today is seen as a landmark in British poetry.

Think of Wordsworth and you probably think of Dove Cottage at Grasmere, where he settled in 1800 with Dorothy. Coleridge moved up to Keswick and they remained friends for many years. In 1802 William married and a year later the first of his children was born.

Would-be poet, Thomas de Quincey, was a great admirer of both Coleridge and Wordsworth and travelled to the Lakes to meet them, ending up staying with the Wordsworths at Dove Cottage, eventually taking over the tenancy when they moved to Allen Bank on the other side of Grasmere. De Quincey later became editor of the newspaper, *The Westmorland Gazette*, as well as becoming hopelessly addicted to opium.

Meanwhile, Coleridge, whose marriage was in tatters, moved to Allen Bank and stayed with the Wordsworths for eighteen months, finally leaving after a bit of a showdown with William, who disapproved of his increasing dependence on drugs and alcohol. Coleridge left the Lakes and moved to London, where he died in 1834.

The Wordsworths, in their search for a home they liked, lived for a while in Grasmere vicarage, later moving a few miles out of the village to Rydal Mount. (Open to the public). In 1843 William became Poet Laureate on the death of fellow Lakeland poet, Robert Southey. Southey and his family had shared Greta Hall with Coleridge's abandoned wife and children. William died at Rydal in 1850 and was buried in a plot he had chosen in the corner of Grasmere churchyard, with the rest of his family now beside him.

Beatrix Potter

This lady is famous all over the world as the creator of Peter Rabbit, Benjamin Bunny and a whole host of other animal stars. She was born in 1866 in London, the daughter of rich and somewhat repressive parents. The family spent long summer holidays in the Lakes, from which the young Beatrix would bring home small animals she had found, such as a hedgehog she called Mrs Tiggy Winkle, which she would dress up and draw. These drawings led to her paying for the first publication, in 1901, of 'The Tale of Peter Rabbit'. It cost £11 for 250 copies. They sold well, securing her a publishing contract with Frederick Warne, who had previously rejected her, and establishing her as a writer and illustrator.

In 1905, with money from her books she bought 'Hill Top Farm', but only managed to stay there occasionally, remaining at home with her overbearing parents for most of each year.

As her wealth increased she bought up more land, more properties (donating many to the newly formed National Trust) and turned to sheep farming. She married a Hawkshead solicitor (a marriage which her parents strongly opposed) and they moved into a larger house just opposite Hill Top. She died in 1943 at the age of 77. Hill Top remains a carefully preserved museum and is owned by the National Trust.

Alfred Wainwright

Every hardened walker in the Lakes must know the name Wainwright. How many people dip into his guides for advice on the best ascent of a mountain? He wrote and illustrated dozens of books, but by far the most popular is the seven-book set: 'A Pictorial Guide to the Lakeland Fells'. They are the fellwalker's bibles.

Wainwright was born in Lancashire and given the name Alfred, which he detested. He was 23 before he could afford his first holiday and he spent the precious week walking with his cousin in the Lakes, only sixty miles from his home, but he had never been before and was overwhelmed by the beauty of the landscape.

In 1941 he came to work in Kendal, becoming borough treasurer in 1948. He walked alone over the fells and spent the dark nights at his fireside making pen and ink sketches of the places he had visited. He set himself the task of climbing every peak in the Lake District, a task which he estimated would take 13 years. Eventually he decided to start producing books, not for others, but for his own enjoyment; books of his sketches and his intricate maps. In time, as with Beatrix Potter, this led him to financing the first printing before he hooked the attention of a publisher, in this case Westmorland Gazette.

The books eventually earned him a small fortune, none of which he wanted, so he gave it to animal sanctuaries. Today, 40 years since the publication of the first title, the books have not dated and are still popular.

He remained in Kendal with his second wife, Betty, until his death in January 1991. He had recently completed what he vowed would be his final book, 'Wainwright in the Valleys of Lakeland', which in many ways reads as a lament for his younger days on the fells, when the world wasn't quite so obsessed with the "motor car". The unhappy introduction to 'Valleys' was found in his typewriter and must have been the last thing he wrote. In accordance with his wishes, his ashes were scattered on his favourite fell, Haystacks, close to Buttermere; Haystacks is Wainwright's mountain.

John Ruskin

Victorian artist, critic, writer and social reformer, Ruskin lived for nearly 30 years at 'Brantwood' on the eastern shore of Coniston Water. Towards the end of his life he suffered from mental fatigue, depression and delusions. He sat in his wheelchair looking out over the lake, fascinated by the changes in the water. He was buried in Coniston, where his grave is decorated by a Celtic cross. His home, 'Brantwood', overlooking Coniston Water is open to the public.

Arthur Ransome

The author of the celebrated 'Swallows and Amazons' children's books, Ransom lived in various houses around the southern Lakes, and set many of his stories on Coniston Water and Windermere. He is buried at Rusland Church, between the two lakes.

Sir Hugh Walpole

Walpole lived on the western shore of Derwent Water from 1932 until his death in 1941. He was famous for his 'Herries Chronicles' novels published in the early 'Thirties, which are now no longer in demand with the book-buying public. He is buried in Keswick.

Canon Rawnsley

The good Canon (1851-1920) was the vicar of Saint Kentigern's church at Crossthwaite, just outside Keswick, but he was so much more than just a vicar; a friend of Beatrix Potter, a follower of Ruskin, an admirer of Wordsworth, a conservationist, preservationist, and joint-founder of the National Trust. No matter where you go in the Lakes, the chances are Canon Rawnsley had something to do with saving something in the locality for future generations. He was responsible for the placing of many monuments and memorials throughout the district. Quite rightly, there is a memorial to him on Friar's Crag, overlooking Derwent Water.

Film director **Ken Russell** lives near Keswick and likes to put on loud classical music, throw open the windows and gaze out at Skiddaw.

TV presenter, **Melvyn Bragg**, was born in the Lakes, and wrote the best-selling novel, 'The Maid of Buttermere' based on a true story. He has a home in the remote hamlet of High Ireby, north of Bassenthwaite Lake.

Mountaineer, **Chris Bonington**, has lived for many years near Caldbeck, and regularly walks up Skiddaw to keep himself in shape.

I'm not famous and I don't live in the Lake District . . . yet!

Facts about The Lake District

❏ The Lake District is the largest of the National Parks, covering 880 square miles, and was set up in 1951.

❏ The National Trust is the largest landowner in the Lakes and owns almost a quarter of the National Park.

❏ Scafell Pike is the highest point in England (977 metres above sea level).

❑ Helvellyn is the most-climbed mountain in England (949 metres above sea level).

❑ 90% of all visitors to the Lakes come by car.

❑ 14.5 million people live within 3 hours' drive.

❑ The county of Cumbria was formed as recently as 1974, prior to which the area had been split between Cumberland, Westmorland and Lancashire.

❑ Windermere is the largest lake in England (over 10.5 miles long).

❑ Derwent Water is the widest of the 16 lakes (1.5 miles) but has an average depth of only 18 feet.

❑ Wastwater is the deepest lake: 258 feet at its deepest.

❑ For some reason, Sellafield attracts approximately 200,000 visitors annually, whereas Wordsworth's home, Dove Cottage, attracts only 80,000, and Beatrix Potter's home, Hill Top, attracts 70,000.

❑ Rainfall varies drastically within the region due to the mountains. Seathwaite in Borrowdale is the wettest place to be (reputed to have the highest annual rainfall in the whole of Britain) having an average of 131 inches a year, whereas Keswick, only a few miles away collects only 58 inches. By comparison, the people of Carlisle must be laughing; they receive only an annual total of 31 inches.

❑ In 1967 Donald Campbell died on Coniston Water in his boat, 'Bluebird', while trying to break the World Water Speed record. His body, along with the majority of the wreckage, was never found.

❑ The National Park has a steady population of 41,000.

❑ Ennerdale Water is the only lake without a road along at least one of its shores. It can be reached only by foot (or horse or CYCLE!) and is therefore the most remote of the lakes.

❑ Perhaps surprisingly, farming is no longer the principal employer. The largest employer by far is . . . the tourist industry.

The Southern and Central Lakes

CLAPPERSGATE TO SAWREY

THROUGH BEATRIX POTTER COUNTRY

Starting point: Either main car park, Ambleside (NY375046) or Under Loughrigg (NY371044).

Distance: 20 miles (14 miles by ferries).

Terrain: Roads on the way there, bridleways on the way back, which are rough in places (can be avoided by taking the Windermere ferry).

Maps: OS Landranger 90; OS Outdoor Leisure 7; OS Touring Map 3.

Public Toilets: Hawkshead, near to car park. There are toilets at 'Hill Top' for visitors to house only.

Refreshments: The Drunken Duck Inn between Skelwith/Outgate; The Outgate inn, Outgate. Hawkshead: cafés, pubs, restaurants. Near Sawrey: café, pub.

This is a relatively easy circuit. There are a couple of hills, but not so severe that you should have to dismount. The countryside is mixed woodland and picturesque villages on the way there, and a shore-line ride across rough terrain on the way back, along a bridleway popular with mountain bikers. This can be managed without too much trouble by ordinary cycles, though it may be a bit bone-jarring in places and preferable to walk short distances over rocky areas. An alternative return can be made using the Windermere ferries.

✦ If you are starting from Ambleside, follow the signs for the A593 to Coniston. Clappersgate is about 1 mile along that road.

Clappersgate is a pleasant hamlet of small cottages centred around a large white building, formerly a hotel, which can be seen for miles along Windermere, and is now split into private apartments. There is a footpath next to the Phone Box leading up to Todd Crag, an unbeatable vantage point taking in the head of Windermere and much of the surrounding countryside.

✦ The route begins a quarter of a mile after the village. If you are driving, there is a small lay-by for parking on the left by a row of beech trees. Cross the footbridge over the River Brathay and bear right along the lane.

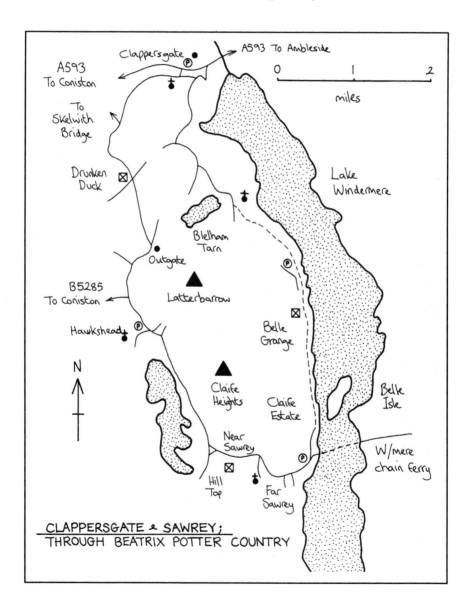

CLAPPERSGATE & SAWREY;
THROUGH BEATRIX POTTER COUNTRY

Romanesque-style Brathay church on the left of the lane was built in the 1830s, the site of which Wordsworth helped to choose. Of the setting he wrote: "There is no situation outside the Alps or among them more beautiful."

✦ Continue along the narrow lane which follows the course of the river for a short way and then starts to rise. At the hamlet of Skelwith Fold keep left – pay attention here as the road markings may not be clearly visible and a wrong turn will lose you valuable height. The road becomes quite steep, but only for a short way. Keep left at the next junction and continue up to the Drunken Duck inn at the crossroads.

Lakeland Cottages: Skelwith Fold

There are seats outside the inn from which there are good views north-east to Ambleside and its surrounding fells.

✦ Head straight across at the crossroads (the good views continue for a short way). Follow the road which leads down to the village of Outgate.

The old village water pump stands on the corner in its protective stone shelter. The only working pumps you'll find in Outgate today are those along the bar of The Outgate inn opposite.

The residents of the very photogenic white-walled cottages deserve an award for their efforts at enhancing their homes even further with the addition of hanging baskets and trained roses. Surely it's time Outgate won the *Best Kept Village* award.

✦ Turn right onto the B5286 and climb the gentle rise from Outgate, after which it is mainly downhill all the way to Hawkshead. The road skirts the centre of the village. If you want to stop bear right for the car parks. There are railings by the telephone boxes where you can chain your bike.

Hawkshead is definitely worth a visit, which is probably why it's always busy. Wordsworth attended the minute grammar school next to the church (open to the public daily March to October) where he began writing poetry. From the church of Saint Michael there are excellent views of the surrounding countryside to the fells beyond Ambleside. In the village itself is the Beatrix Potter Gallery (National Trust) housed in what was her solicitor husband's office, where the original watercolours for her famous stories are on display (open Monday to Friday, April to October).

Hawkshead has many gift shops along its narrow cobbled streets and interconnecting courtyards, as well as several pubs, countless cafés, tearooms, restaurants and hotels. There are toilets close to the car park; the only public ones along the entire route.

✦ From Hawkshead return to the B-road, turning left at the T-junction, signed for 'Sawrey & Windermere via ferry'. This will take you along the eastern shore of Esthwaite Water to Near Sawrey (2.5 miles).

This pleasant road is relatively flat and keeps close to the lake for most of the way. There is access to the shore about half-way along.

The road becomes steeper as it draws towards Near Sawrey: a cluster of white and grey houses, not exactly a postcard village, but nice enough. There is a café and a small pub, 'The Tower Bank Arms', owned by the National Trust, and featured in 'The Tale of Jemima Puddleduck'. The reason everyone flocks to the village is to visit 'Hill Top', the home of Beatrix Potter, now also National Trust owned and run (open April to October, daily except Thursday and Friday). Hill Top is towards the end of the village on the right, with a small area for parking, or more rightly 'chaining up', opposite. The house from the outside is unimpressive, but inside it is a carefully preserved museum containing many of Beatrix Potter's much-loved possessions, including grandfather clocks, plates and furniture.

✦ Follow the road from Near Sawrey to its sister hamlet, Far Sawrey (1 mile).

There is a small but well-stocked village store down a narrow lane to the right (visible from the road) then the Claife Crier Bar on the left, with the adjoining 'Sawrey Hotel'.

✦ The road climbs slightly after the hotel, then drops quite steeply towards windermere. **Beware of tight bends**. This road levels out and runs along the edge of the lake. Take the narrow turning on the left after the National Trust car park.

OR . . . If you want to avoid the rough ride ahead, you could take the chain ferry across the lake (the cost for cyclists is minimal) to experience some of the tourist delights of Windermere and Bowness: restaurants, cafés, gift shops, boat hire, steamboat museum and a more recent attraction which is generating a lot of interest is the 'World of Beatrix Potter' high-tech multi-media display including two short films looking at the life and work of the author. Open daily. To return to Ambleside take the steam cruiser from Bowness pier.

✦ For the bridleway continue along the narrow lane alongside the shore of the lake. Cross the cattle grid into the Claife Heights estate (National Trust).

Claife Heights is the rising expanse of conifers on the left which divides Windermere and Esthwaite Water. Beatrix Potter often used to walk here, though it was less densely forested then. Bridleways through the trees lead back to the Sawreys and Hawkshead.

On the right there are several stoney beaches suitable for picnics. The large island visible from here, Windermere's largest, is Belle Isle, famous for its round house, reputed to be the first, or only true circular house in England.

✦ Over a second cattle grid and the road becomes a stoney trackway, still easily cycleable in its early stages, but it does get worse in places and becomes quite rocky.

If you have a helmet, so much the better, if not, take extra care and walk where necessary over the worst parts. The woods are an ideal place to walk anyway, with occasional views over the lake.

✦ After 2 miles you should come to a house, 'Belle Grange' on the left, at which point several paths lead off in each direction. Stick to the main, central track heading in a northerly direction. This will soon become a gravel driveway. Pass between a set of stone gateposts and bear immediately right through a small National Trust car park and continue along the lakeside track. After about 1 mile this veers away from the water's edge and is sign posted for Wray church, climbing slightly and liable to be muddy in places. When you reach the lane at the top, turn right past the church.

Saint Margaret's of Low Wray is a small, grey, angular church, built in 1856 by a retired Liverpool surgeon, who also built nearby Wray Castle. Here you will find the grave of Canon Rawnsley, one of the founders of the National Trust and a friend of Beatrix Potter, encouraging her to continue with her writing and drawing when no-one else wanted to know.

Back to the road, and next on the right is the castellated gateway to Wray Castle, a 19th century sham, home of the afore-mentioned wealthy surgeon. It is now owned by the National Trust (who else?) and leased to the Navy, who use it as a training centre for radio officers. The grounds are open to the public (access is free) and lead down to the lake. There are paths through mixed woodlands and good views towards Ambleside and Loughrigg Fell.

✦ Continue along the lane, dropping steadily at first, then undulating gently. After 1 mile bear right onto the B-road, heading towards Ambleside. The road becomes enclosed by woodlands on either side. When they end, Brathay church should come into view over on the left. Either take the narrow turning to the left which runs alongside the river to the footbridge, or carry on ahead, crossing over the river to join the main road, bearing right for Ambleside.

GRASMERE

THE WORDSWORTH ROUTE

Starting point: Ideally start from the small Pelter Bridge car park, near Rydal Water (NY366059) but anywhere around the route will suffice.

Distance: 10 to 15 miles, depending on route taken.

Terrain: Roads and bridleways; some walking necessary, difficult in parts.

Maps: OS Landranger 90; OS Outdoor Leisure 7; OS Touring Map 3

Public Toilets: Rothay Park, Ambleside, Grasmere village

Refreshments: Ambleside: cafés, restaurants, pubs. Grasmere: cafés, restaurants, pubs. Dove Cottage: tea room. Rydal Hall: tea shop behind hall

This route passes three of Wordsworth's homes, including the renowned Dove Cottage, and makes use of two bridleways which were regular walks for the poet and his sister Dorothy. As with most of the bridleways in the area they are craggy in parts and for some small stretches cycles will have to be wheeled and at a couple of points lifted over rocky outcrops, but it is a memorable route and the views are so good that these small inconveniences are very worthwhile. The bridleways can be avoided by using the roads, but take care on the A591 which is busy for most of the day.

✦ From Ambleside: if you have a car, either park it in the town's main car park (signposted) and follow the signs around the one way system heading for the A593 Coniston road. Once over the narrow stone bridge that crosses the River Rothay take the first right turning, signposted 'Under Loughrigg'. There is also parking further along this road on the right, which makes a convenient place to begin from. Follow the lane, but beware of approaching traffic and/or pedestrians.

Half a mile along this pleasant lane, after the parked cars is a hump-backed bridge crossing the river and leading to Ambleside's

Rothay Park, which has a good playground if you happen to be with children. The lane skirts the lower slopes of Loughrigg Fell and any of the footpaths leading off to the left makes an interesting walk, leading to good views of Windermere, Rydal Water or Grasmere, depending on how far you continue.

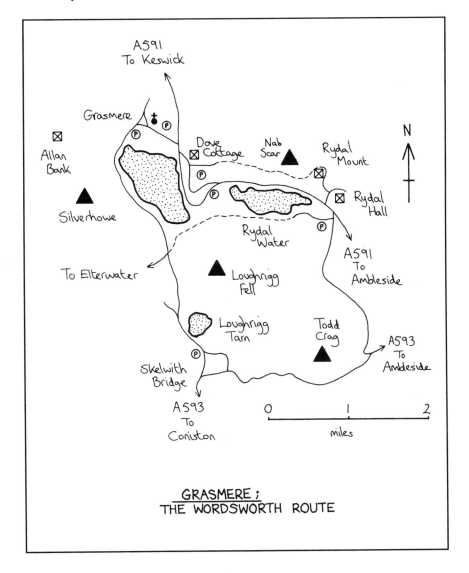

GRASMERE :
THE WORDSWORTH ROUTE

About a mile from the bridge, notice on the left 'Fox Ghyll', where poet and Wordsworth admirer, Thomas de Quincey, lived for a time. A little further along on the same side is 'Loughrigg Holme' where Wordsworth's daughter, Dora, and her husband lived. A little further still is a house called 'Stepping Stones' which was once owned by Wordsworth's son, also named William. The house, not surprisingly, overlooks a set of stepping stones crossing the Rothay, leading back towards Ambleside.

◆ Cross the cattle grid after 'Stepping Stones' and follow the road across an area of open pasture. Ahead is Pelter Bridge, crossing the river and leading to the main road. Take the lane to the left, immediately before the bridge. On the left is the Pelter Bridge car park. Continue along the narrow lane leading uphill for half a mile to Rydal Water.

There are benches here if you want to rest, picnic, or just take in the excellent views over the lake. Rydal Water has two main islands. On one of them Sir William le Fleming of Rydal Hall decided to build a summer house, but abandoned the idea when he found out it was possible to wade out to it. That said, the lake is 55 feet at its deepest, so watch where you wade should you choose to attempt it.

The craggy fell on the opposite side of the water is Nab Scar, at the foot of which stands Nab Cottage, a long white homestead built in 1702, another one-time home of poet and opium addict, Thomas de Quincey, also once the home of Coleridge's son, Hartley, and now a guesthouse.

Rydal was originally 'Rye-dale': the dale where rye is grown. No rye is grown in Rydal today.

◆ The bridleway runs for half a mile along the water's edge before veering away uphill. It may be necessary to walk some stretches. Between the Rydal and Grasmere lakes there are several paths to choose from, but keep to the upper one which is the bridleway and leads to Loughrigg Terrace. This is flatter and easily manageable, but it is narrow, so have consideration for pedestrians and horses.

'Loughrigg' means 'the ridge above the lake'. The terrace offers its famous, much-photographed, much-painted view over Grasmere towards Silverhowe and Helm Crag. There are several well-placed benches along the way, where the weary cyclist can rest and enjoy the scenery. Towards the end of the terrace are routes up to the summit of

Loughrigg Fell, of which Wainwright wrote: "No ascent is more repaying for the small labour involved" – in other words, it's well worth the climb.

✦ Through the gate at the end of the terrace, a clear trackway leads through the National Trust woods to a lane. Turn right and follow the road downhill into Grasmere village (2 miles) but take care as the road is steep and bends repeatedly. At the top of the descent is a sign warning cyclists to dismount for the first steep drop. Do not ignore this or you are liable to end up bruised, broken or buried.

There are many worthy short walks in this area. Footpaths to the right lead to the lake, while those on the left lead up through woodlands to more mountainous country, principally the table-top plateau of Silver-howe (or Silver How) from which there are unsurpassed views over the two lakes.

Rowing boats are available for hire on Grasmere just before you enter the village. On the left at this point, standing alone beyond the fields, is Allen Bank, where Wordsworth and his family lived for three years after Dove Cottage became too small.

Look out for the car park on the right (next to the Tourist Information Centre) which is a suitable place to leave your bike if you intend to explore the village on foot and sample one (or all) of its cafés or hostelries. The Rowan Tree café and restaurant occupies a site that for centuries has housed a place of refreshment. Its outside tables look over the River Rothay to the grey tower of Saint Oswald's. The church is rather drab on the outside but the interior is quite the reverse. A 'rush-bearing ceremony' still takes place every year, harking back to the days when the church had no proper floor, and rushes were laid down over the earth like a carpet. The Wordsworth family graves can be found in the corner of the graveyard, close to the river: a spot chosen by the poet himself.

Grasmere is literally (no pun intended) littered with references to Wordsworth: 'The Wordsworth Hotel', 'The Prelude Restaurant', 'The Wild Daffodil' tea room. The shops are full of his poetry, his 'Guide to the Lakes' and postcards of Dove Cottage. It is undeniably a tourist village, but there is nothing brash or ostentatious about it.

Amongst the many shops in the village, there is the Lakeland Perfumery, where perfumes are named after local fells and villages. Directly opposite, next to the chapel, are the public toilets. To the right and over the village green are the Heaton-Cooper Studios, exhibiting paintings of the surrounding landscape by the famous family of artists. The village hall also usually has some sort of exhibition on and charges a nominal entrance fee.

✦ From the car park turn right towards the church, then right again at the junction, crossing over the river and passing a final section of gift shops and cafes, until fields open out on either side and you come to the main road. Take the narrow lane almost directly opposite.

This is still Grasmere, a detached section of the village called Town End. Here you will find the tiny Dove Cottage, Wordsworth's most famous home, where he lived for eight years (1800-1808) and wrote his most famous works. It was here that his sister, Dorothy, kept her journal: a vivid account of their daily life and of the natural history of the area.

The cottage was built before 1617 and was originally an inn called The Dove and Olive Branch. When the Wordsworths left for Allan Bank, Thomas de Quincey took over the tenancy.

Dove Cottage attracts visitors from all over the world: America, Japan and endless streams of Germans. There is now also a Wordsworth museum next door, along with a gift shop, a tea room and even (some call it enterprising, some call it commercialism) a Dove Cottage guest-house. It makes you wonder what Wordsworth himself would have to say about it all.

✦ Continue along the lane past Dove Cottage, which rises steadily. To avoid the bridleway continue straight ahead, bearing left onto the A591 and take the left after rydal water for rydal mount. For the bridleway take the first left turning after Dove Cottage, leading very steeply uphill for a short way, signed as 'unsuitable for motors' (there is a bench on the left if you want a brief rest, from which there are good views over Grasmere to Silverhowe). The road soon levels out and becomes a gravel trackway. Other paths and tracks lead off, but keep to the main, central trackway.

Nab Scar is the rocky crag ahead, around the base of which this bridleway skirts. There are good views across Rydal Water to the bulk of Loughrigg Fell. You should be able to see the jagged mouth of Rydal Cave, sinking back into the hillside: a huge cavern, which, Wainwright says, is so big it could hold the entire population of Ambleside. It is part of a long abandoned blue slate quarry on the fell. As if to prove it, shards of discarded slate form screes outside its entrance.

Rydal Water and Loughrigg Fell

✦ Continue along the trackway, which at certain points will be impassable to the cyclist and it will be necessary to wheel your bike over the rocky areas (pity the poor horses that have to negotiate this path with someone sitting on their backs!) After the worst of the craggy areas there looks to be a pathway to the left which has been shored up with stone. This **is not** a path and leads only to loose scree. Here, another path leads down to the main road and White Moss Common, while the bridleway continues ahead, much gentler from now on. Go through the gate where there is a stone bench ahead looking over to the lake.

This bridleway, like Loughrigg Terrace, was another of Wordsworth's favourite walks, as it afforded "very favourable views of the lake and the vale". The views are still excellent, and apart from occasional glimpses of the traffic on the main road below it is essentially unchanged since the poet's day.

✦ Continue along the track which passes directly behind Rydal Mount and emerges onto a steep road. Bear right for the house.

The Wordsworths moved into Rydal Mount in 1813, and William, his wife Mary and his sister Dorothy, all remained here until their deaths. William himself landscaped the gardens, building terraces and steps, from which you can see Windermere in the distance. The house is a pleasing and sturdy structure in a perfect setting. The only bad thing that now affects it is the sound of the main road which filters up through the trees. William became Poet Laureate while living here and the house saw many famous guests. The Wordsworths began to rub shoulders with the nobility.

There is a notice in William's study declaring that he last climbed Helvellyn at the age of 74. An impressive feat at that age. He died in 1850, shortly after his 80th birthday, having contracted pleurisy after a walk on White Moss Common.

Further down the steep lane towards the main road is the church of Saint Mary, built in 1823 by Lady le Fleming of Rydal Hall, who leased Rydal Mount to the Wordsworths. Through the church yard you can reach the National Trust owned woodland 'Dora's Field'. In 1826 the le Flemings tried to oust the Wordsworths from Rydal Mount because they wanted the house for a relative, so William bought this plot of vacant land close to the church and threatened to build himself a house on it, which would ruin the outlook from Rydal Mount. The le Flemings gave in and William gave the land to his daughter, Dora. The spring is the best time to visit, when all the daffodils are in bloom.

Also of interest in Rydal, is the home of the le Flemings themselves: Rydal Hall, which stands opposite Rydal Mount. The hall is private, but the gardens are open daily to the public.

On the left behind the hall is a driveway, leading off which there is a footpath to Rydal Falls. A little further along the driveway is a small tea room, rather bare and basic, but one of its nice features is that in good weather you can sit outside next to the waters of Rydal Beck. The track continues to a pleasant area of parkland, which was yet another of Wordsworth's favourite places. Of the parkland he wrote that it was "made by nature for herself". He often came here to compose his poems and for romantic walks with his wife.

✦ From Rydal, drop down the steep lane past the church and bear left onto the main road. After a quarter of a mile turn right over Pelter Bridge, crossing the River Brathay and bear right to the car park.

✦ To extend the route and take in Loughrigg Tarn, turn right out of the car park and right along Under Loughrigg (described earlier in this section) follow the lane alongside the river and turn right onto the A593. Continue through the hamlet of Clappersgate towards Skelwith Bridge. The road undulates but is without any strenuous climbs. Take care on the tight corners. Take the first right turning, which winds uphill.

As the road levels towards the top there is a footpath off to the right to Loughrigg Tarn (strictly no cycles, so explore it on foot). Wordsworth was very fond of the tarn, and described it as "Diana's looking glass . . . round, clear and bright as heaven." There are excellent views all the way around the water, especially of "those lusty twins", the Langdale Pikes, clearly visible in the distance.

The Langdale Pikes across Loughrigg Tarn

✦ Follow the road to the right around the tarn. Keep right.

The first left turning after the tarn leads to Elterwater (pub, general store) and back to Skelwith Bridge (pub, cafés). The road around the tarn passes between farm buildings and heads steadily uphill with Loughrigg Fell on the right. On the left is the National Trust's 'High Close Estate', the grounds lead up to the High Close Youth Hostel. The next turning on the left leads to the Youth Hostel and Elterwater. Almost opposite on the right is the gate leading to Loughrigg Terrace, after which it drops steeply to Grasmere.

✦ Either return via the terrace or continue into Grasmere. From Grasmere the A591 can be followed back to Pelter Bridge and the car park.

ELTERWATER & THE LANGDALES

TO THE SOURCE OF THE BRATHAY

Starting points: Skelwith Bridge (NY344034). Elterwater village (NY329049)

Distance: From Skelwith Bridge 15 miles. From Elterwater 12 miles

Terrain: Undulating roads with two steep climbs

Time: From Skelwith Bridge 4 hours; from Elterwater, $3^1/_2$ hours

Maps: OS Landranger 90; OS Outdoor Leisure 6 & 7; OS Touring Map 3

Public Toilets: Elterwater village, near National Trust car park; Stickle Ghyll National Trust car park, Great Langdale

Refreshments: A surprising number of places exist along the Great Langdale road, among the best are:Chesters (coffee shop), Kirkstone Gallery Skelwith Bridge; The Rosewood Tea Garden, over the river from the car park; The Talbot Bar, Skelwith Bridge; Britannia Inn, Elterwater; The Stickle Barn, Great Langdale (Through Stickle Ghyll car park); after Great Langdale there is only the Three Shires Inn, Little Langdale

---

✦ If you are cycling from Ambleside, follow the signs for the A593 Coniston road. This road is often busy and has several tight bends, so keep well in. The road follows the course of the River Brathay upstream. Skelwith Bridge is just under 3 miles. Bear right onto the B5343 for Elterwater, a further 2.5 miles.

This route takes in both of the vastly different Langdale valleys and is gently undulating for most of the way, with two steep climbs. There is limited parking at Skelwith Bridge next to the river. If these spaces are full, continue along the B5343 Great Langdale Road, where there is a National Trust car park after half a mile on the right, or continue to Elterwater, where there are various car parks in and around the village.

Skelwith Bridge is a hamlet which has grown up around, not surprisingly, a bridge. Among the little huddle of buildings is a hotel with its accompanying Talbot Bar around the rear. Close to the river you'll see slate picnic tables and a crop of curious standing stones, courtesy of the Kirkstone Slate Gallery, who have workshops and a showroom along the driveway here, and more importantly, a pleasant slate-floored coffee shop and restaurant called 'Chesters', which is well worth a visit either at the start or finish of your ride, or preferably both.

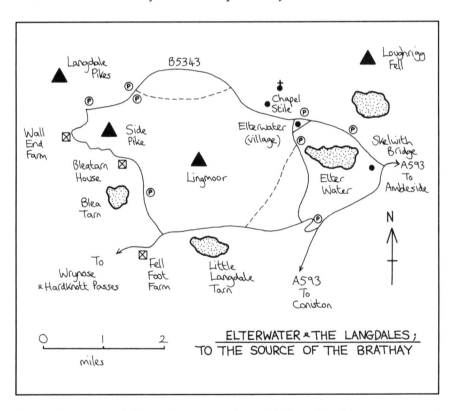

ELTERWATER & THE LANGDALES;
TO THE SOURCE OF THE BRATHAY

If you leave your bike in the car park and follow the driveway around the side of Chesters and between the slate workshops (where slate cutting, polishing and shaping will more than likely be in progress) you will come to a wooded pathway alongside the River Brathay. In a couple of hundred yards you will see the Skelwith Falls waterfall. The drop is only sixteen feet, which is nothing for Lakeland, but the force has the impressive distinction of carrying a greater volume of water that any other falls in the National Park. After rain the force can increase drastically and the valley bottom around Skelwith is prone to flooding, hardly surprising really, as the Brathay collects all the water from both Great and Little Langdale and their surrounding fells – a fair amount of water.

Another well-known beauty spot near Skelwith Bridge is picturesque Loughrigg Tarn. The footpath opposite the Talbot Bar will take you there in just under a mile, as will the steep lane just to the right. The tarn is well worth a visit, being an idyllic spot, remaining essentially unchanged since Wordsworth's day. It was one of the poet's favourite places and he referred to it as "Diana's looking glass . . . round, clear and bright as heaven"

Loughrigg Tarn and Fell

From the road side there is the much-photographed view of reeds, water-lilies and a white-walled Lakeland cottage, with Loughrigg Fell in the background. From the other side is an equally worthy view across the water to the Langdale Pikes in the distance, which appear from here as two solid dome-shaped peaks: Wordsworth's "lusty twins".

✦ From Skelwith Bridge follow the B-road behind the hotel (B5343) towards Elterwater (2.5 miles).

There are views over Elterwater (the lake) on the left, with the unmistakable Langdale Pikes visible again across the water, dominating any view towards Great Langdale, often scraping the cloud layer and sometimes lost altogether.

Elterwater (the village) nestles in the bottom of the valley, built largely of local slate. The grey scars of quarrying can be seen just behind the village. Once the home of a gunpowder factory, Elterwater is now a sleepy little place with a few B & Bs, a youth hostel, a general store and the renowned Britannia Inn overlooking the village green, a pleasant place to stop for refreshment of the liquid variety, especially on a sunny afternoon or warm evening.

The River Brathay cuts across the bottom of the village. Looking over the stone bridge you can see the water is crystal clear, flowing over a bed of grey-green slate. Close to the bridge is the riverside path that leads to Skelwith Bridge via Elterwater lake.

It is generally accepted that there are sixteen lakes in Lakeland (the many lesser expanses of water being classed as tarns) and that Elterwater is the smallest of the sixteen. It is just half a mile across and very oddly shaped, though most of it is inaccessible and some of it hidden from view behind trees and reeds. 'Elterwater' is old Norse for 'Swan Lake'. There are often pairs of swans to be seen eyeing the passing ramblers with distaste.

✦ From Elterwater village return to the B-road and bear left. Continue past 'Wainwright's Inn' on the left and then through the village of Chapel Stile.

There is a good village store on the right near the beginning of the village if you want to replenish your stock of drinks etc. After Chapel Stile the valley opens out and Great Langdale begins: a glaciated valley, formed during the ice ages. The fell on the left, over the river, is Lingmoor. ('Ling' means heather). Fellwalker Wainwright assures us that the top of Lingmoor Fell is the best place for "appraising the geography of the Langdale District". What Wainwright says is law to many thousands of keen walkers who flock to the Lakes with his guidebooks tucked into their rucksacks or pockets. On a clear day the views from this relatively small fell are exceptional in all directions. It is well worth an excursion if you have the energy.

✦ Just under a mile after Chapel Stile there is a bridleway on the left with a postbox built into the wall at the corner. This cuts through the valley towards the head of Langdale, but is bumpy in places and can be muddy. Either take the bridleway or continue along the road to Stickle Ghyll National Trust car park. Each has its merits.

The bridleway rejoins the road opposite Stickle Ghyll. From here there are paths up to the Langdale Pikes which tower above, crowning the valley and generally looking pretty impressive. Wainwright says that other places may dim in the memory, but the "distinctive profile" of the Langdale Pikes "leaves an indelible imprint on the mind", and that all days spent on the noble Pikes are "golden days".

A short walk from here will take you to Dungeon Ghyll Force and several clear streams and tempting rock pools: an ideal place for dipping pedal-weary feet.

✦ Continue along the valley road towards the head of the valley.

The Old Dungeon Ghyll Hotel on the right incorporates the famous 'hikers' bar, haunt of the true mountain men. The *Good Pub Guide* describes it as full of character, but "boisterous", so be warned.

✦ After the hotel the road loses its 'B' classification and becomes simply a lane, veering sharply to the left at the junction where the three valleys of Mickleden, Oxendale (both road-free) and Great Langdale meet. Pass the edge of the National Trust campsite on the left and Wall End Farm on the right, after which the road begins to climb steeply. The severe gradient only persists for a short way and is best attempted on foot.

The skyline on the right of the climb is made up of Crinkle Crags and Bowfell, a magnet for the seasoned walker. On the left is a much tamer peak: a rocky crag on the lower slopes of Lingmoor called Side Pike. The short climb to the top is rewarded with fine views across the valleys below and along Great Langdale towards Windermere.

As the road rounds Side Pike, Blea Tarn comes into view, lying low between the fells, seeming remote and secluded. However, it is an attractive and popular little tarn set against a backdrop of rhododendrons and tall pines. There is just one building in sight: the whitewashed stone walls of Bleatarn House, centuries old, now a Bed and Breakfast. The road winds and undulates continually and the mountains on either side can seem sheer and unyielding. Ahead on the left is the Blea Tarn car park. There are paths to the shore and through the coniferous woodlands beyond. An excellent place for a short walk or picnic, with a view northwards of the Langdale Pikes (what else?) displaying all FIVE of the pikes, looking from here like an extinct volcano.

✦ Follow the road as it drops steadily to a T-junction. Turn left.

Or, a brief detour (about half a mile) to the right will take you to Fell Foot Farm, behind which is a barrow-like structure in the field, which is a 'Thing' or 'Ting' Mound, the site of a Viking Parliament. Slightly further along this road you can see several streams, gills or becks cascading down from the Wrynose Pass and its surrounding fells, which all come together to form a youthful River Brathay. Return the same way to the T-junction and continue into Little Langdale.

Little Langdale Tarn on the right, surrounded by fields, is idyllic, perhaps made even more so because there is no public access to its shores. Through it flows the Brathay, later to flow into Skelwith Force, eventually emptying into Windermere.

The valley's only road twists and turns and is very narrow, only one car width in most places, so keep an eye out for on-coming traffic.

Half a mile after the tarn you will come across, on the left, Little Langdale's only pub – The Three Shires Inn – the shires in question being Westmorland, Cumberland and Lancashire, which met close to here before the new county of Cumbria was created. The inn is popular with tourists and has a beer garden at the side and seats beneath a veranda at the front, surrounded by colourful hanging baskets, and offering unspoilt views across the valley.

✦ Continue past the inn, soon after which the road begins to descend for 2 miles.

The road cuts between National Trust woodlands. In the trees on the right is Colwith Force, a waterfall with a drop of some 90 feet. There are several interesting footpaths on both sides of the road which meander over the pastures and between the lone farmhouses, many of which are several hundred years old and are now National Trust owned.

✦ At the T-junction turn left for Elterwater, a pleasant downhill run with glimpses of the lake on the right (2 miles). For Skelwith Bridge turn right, cross over the Brathay and follow the lane which climbs fairly steeply towards the main road. Skelwith Bridge is 1 mile to the left.

On the main road there is a lay-by on the left which gives fine views over the surrounding countryside, particularly the thick woodlands of Little Langdale, through which you have just cycled. As might be expected, the ever-present Langdale Pikes can be seen towering in the background. With such scenery on display it is difficult to take a photograph and NOT get a good picture.

Lingmoor, Little Langdale and the Langdale Pikes

Take care on the approach to Skelwith; there is a tight bend and the bridge is quite narrow. At Skelwith Bridge you can reward yourself at Chesters or the Rosewood Tea Garden.

If you're heading next in the direction of Ambleside and have time to spare, stop in the hamlet of Clappersgate (parking on the right of the road, just before the houses) and take the footpath next to the Phone box, which leads up to Todd Crag. The walk should take half an hour at a leisurely pace. From the Crag, there are unsurpassed views over Windermere. You can see where the River Brathay joins the Rothay (from the Vale of Grasmere) and snakes lazily into the head of Windermere on the last leg of its journey.

ESTHWAITE WATER

HAWKSHEAD TO 'HILL TOP'

Starting point: Hawkshead Car Park (NY354981).

Distance: 7 miles.

Terrain: Roads, relatively easy. No off-road cycling.

Time: 1 hour for a leisurely ride.

Maps: OS Landranger 97; OS Outdoor Leisure 7; OS Touring Map 3.

Public Toilets: Hawkshead car park; Toilets at Hill Top, for visitors to house only.

Refreshments: Hawkshead: pubs, cafés, restaurants. Far Sawrey: pub, café.

This is a short route around Hawkshead's very pleasant lake. The roads are mainly flat with two brief climbs which should not present any problem. Beatrix Potter's home, Hill Top, is at Far Sawrey and is open to the public (currently open Sunday to Wednesday, 11am to 5 pm, Easter to October).

✦ Start from the main car park in Hawkshead. Turn right onto the B-road then left at the junction, signposted 'Sawrey and Windermere via Ferry'.

The road crosses over Black Beck (which runs into Esthwaite Water) then curves around gradually to run along the length of the lake. Wordsworth spent many happy hours here as a boy, walking in the summer, skating in the winter. Beatrix Potter thought Esthwaite Water the most beautiful of all the lakes, and it became the setting for 'The Tale of Mr Jeremy Fisher'.

The only access to the shore on this side is about half way along, with clear paths through the trees, leading to shingle beaches. A pleasant spot to take in the views, though normally frequented by fishermen.

The road is relatively flat for most of the way, until it veers away from the water and climbs slightly just before the village of Near Sawrey,

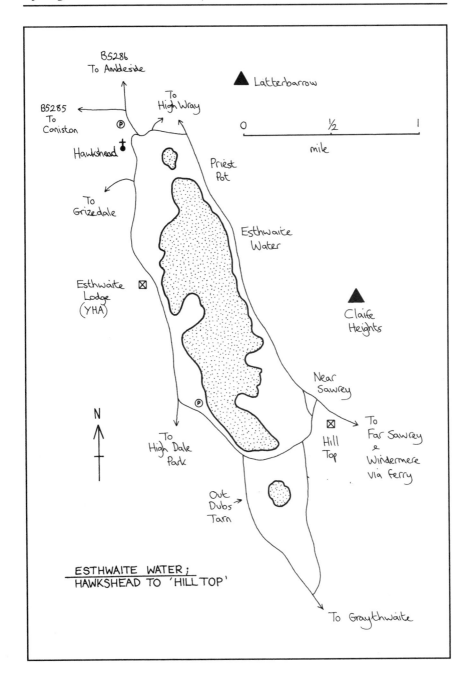

B5286
To Ambleside

Latterbarrow

B5285
To
Coniston

To
High Wray

Ⓟ

Hawkshead

0 ½ 1
mile

Priest
Pot

To
Grizedale

Esthwaite
Water

Esthwaite
Lodge
(YHA) ☒

Claife
Heights

Near
Sawrey

N
↑

To
High Dale
Park

Ⓟ

☒
Hill
Top

To
Far Sawrey
&
Windermere
via ferry

Out
Dubs
Tarn

ESTHWAITE WATER;
HAWKSHEAD TO 'HILLTOP'

To Graythwaite

where Beatrix Potter lived. The village is carefully preserved, so little has changed over the years since Beatrix first bought Hill Top, a grey pebble-dashed farmhouse, now housing a wealth of ornate treasures inside. It is situated at the far end of the village, with a small parking space opposite. It attracts visitors from all over the world and is one of the Lake District's top tourist attractions. As the house is so small there is often a queue awaiting entry.

✦ From Hill Top, return along the same road through the village and take the first left turning, dropping past hotels and houses towards the lake. Either continue on this road and turn right at the T-junction, heading back to Hawkshead, or take the narrow lane to the left which looks at first as if it is about to climb steeply, but is in fact quite flat. This lane heads south, away from the lake, offering good views of the surrounding countryside. In 1 mile you will arrive at a T-junction. Turn right heading back towards Hawkshead (2.5 miles)

In 1.5 miles the road comes close to the bottom of Esthwaite Water where there is a car park and access to the shore. Slightly further along there are boats for hire.

Hawkshead Church and the Central Fells

There is also access to the head of the lake via a footpath close to Hawkshead, leading along a farm driveway to the reed fringed northern reaches. This makes an excellent short walk with fine views, a good place for a picnic before completing the last short leg of the journey back to the village.

✦ On the approach to Hawkshead pass the road close to the church marked 'No Entry' and take the next left back towards the car parks (first turning on the left).

HAWKSHEAD TO LAKESIDE

RANSOME'S LAST DAYS

Starting point: Hawkshead car park (NY354981).

Distance: 30 miles.

Terrain: Tarmac roads; no off-road cycling. Several brief uphill stretches; a few minutes of walking.

Time: 3 hours for a leisurely ride.

Maps: OS Landranger 97; OS Touring Map 3.

Public Toilets: Hawkshead, near car park; Graythwaite Hall: patrons only; Stott Park Bobbin Mill: patrons only; Lakeside: steamer pier.

Refreshments: Hawkshead: cafés, pubs, restaurants. Lakeside steamer pier: café, sweet shop.

✦ To Hawkshead from Ambleside: follow the A593 (to Coniston) out of the town centre. At Clappersgate (1 mile out of Ambleside) turn left along the B5286. This road passes through the village of Outgate and leads directly to Hawkshead. Follow signs to the right for car park.

This route can fit comfortably into a morning or afternoon, but it is worth taking a full day for a more relaxed pace, allowing time for the steeper sections. There are several places of interest along the way: gardens, a museum, chance to ride on a steam train or lake steamer, so adjust your time accordingly.

✦ Leave the car park at Hawkshead, turning right onto the B-road, then left along the eastern shore of Esthwaite water, signposted for 'Sawrey and Windermere via Ferry'. The road climbs very briefly into Near Sawrey. Turn right between hotels and houses, dropping back towards the lake. Take the narrow lane on the left, leading south, away from Esthwaite Water.

(For more information on the lake see the Esthwaite Water circuit.)

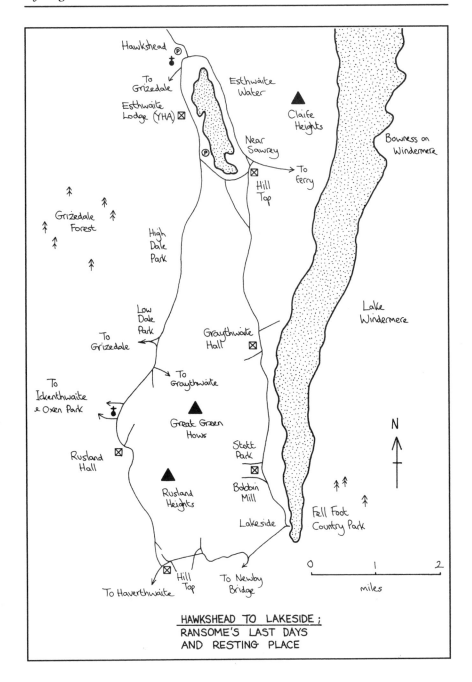

Hawkshead

To Grizedale

Esthwaite Water

Esthwaite Lodge (YHA)

Claife Heights

Bowness on Windermere

Near Sawrey

To Ferry

Hill Top

Grizedale Forest

High Dale Park

Low Dale Park

Lake Windermere

To Grizedale

Graythwaite Hall

To Graythwaite

To Ickenthwaite & Oxen Park

Great Green Hows

Rusland Hall

Stott Park

Rusland Heights

Boddin Mill

Lakeside

Fell Foot Country Park

N

Hill Top

To Haverthwaite

To Newby Bridge

0   1   2

miles

HAWKSHEAD TO LAKESIDE ; RANSOME'S LAST DAYS AND RESTING PLACE

Take care on this lane as it is single track for most of the way. It is worth stopping for a few minutes for the views back over the water and of the surrounding landscape.

✦ At the T-junction turn left. The road rises quite steeply after this (don't worry — it soon levels out). Continue on to Graythwaite Hall (2.5 miles from junction) the driveway to which is on the right, noticeable by its stately wrought iron gates. There is a telephone box on the corner opposite.

The roads on this side of Windermere are usually fairly quiet. At certain times of day you can cycle around for hours without passing a soul. Even at their busiest these roads have nothing like the volume of traffic as roads on the opposite shore. The area is largely unspoilt: mixed woodland and coniferous forest, with very few houses and even fewer villages.

Graythwaite Hall gardens are open daily from 10 o'clock. Payment is by an honesty box in the car park at the end of the winding driveway. The hall (not open) was built in the 18th century, being enlarged and re-faced several times over the years, and is now in the Victorian Gothic style. The six-acre gardens have a pond, rose garden and arboretum. There are toilets on site for visitors. It was in the woods surrounding the grounds that Wordsworth, while schooling at Hawkshead Grammar, used to walk and collect hazelnuts.

✦ From the hall, continue along the lane, downhill to Low Stott park (3 miles).

There is very little access to the shore of Windermere on this side of the lake, the majority of the land being privately owned. There is, however, a footpath just under 1.5 miles from Graythwaite Hall which leads in half a mile to the bank close to the little tree-covered island of Silverholme, which was Arthur Ransome's Cormorant Island of 'Swallows and Amazons' fame.

Stott Park Bobbin Mill is on the right at the start of the hamlet of Low Stott Park. It is a restored water-powered mill which made bobbins from timber cut from local woods. It is open daily from April to October.

✦ Continue along the road through Low Stott Park, dropping down between some very 'desirable' residences to Lakeside. Bear left for the steamer and railway car park on the waterfront.

As well as its large hotel, Lakeside offers toilets, a tuck shop and cafeteria with lake views, all at the steamer terminal. From here you can take a steamer to Bowness, Ambleside, or a round trip back to Lakeside. Cycles are half fare, dependent on destination. Check current prices at booking office or any Tourist Information Centre.

There is also a passenger ferry across the lake to the National Trust's Fell Foot Country Park, where there are waterside walks, gardens, café and toilets.

Behind the steamboat terminus is the start of the Haverthwaite and Lakeside Railway, which will take you to Haverthwaite, three miles away on a steam train, and then return you to Lakeside.

✦ From the steamer car park return to the road and turn left. After 1 mile the road crosses the steam railway. Take the right turning immediately after the railway bridge. The road travels for a short way close to the rails, then crosses them once again. There are now woodlands on either side and the road begins a steep, but brief climb. Unless you get a good run up it may be necessary to dismount. Take the next left then the immediate right. Follow this road which soon descends.

On the left just before the steep drop is Hill Top (not to be confused with its namesake in Sawrey, where Beatrix Potter lived). This was the final home of Arthur Ransome, where he worked on his autobiography, which was published posthumously. He and his Russian wife bought the house in 1960, but Ransome became ill and was moved to hospital, where he died peacefully in 1967. The house is now a kennels.

✦ Take the next right for Rusland (3 miles).

The road to Rusland is mainly flat, with just a few undulations. This is a quiet valley with deciduous woodland on the right and attractive pastures and good views of the forested Grizedale area on the left. The magnificent frontage of Rusland Hall can be seen over a mile away: an early Georgian building which, until recent years, was open to the public, but maintenance costs were too high and the hall was sold and converted into private apartments.

✦ Turn left towards the hall, signed 'Oxen Park & Ulverston'. The road passes behind the hall and veers sharply to the right. Follow the road towards Rusland church, avoiding the right turning before the church continue on the road which veers to the left, taking the right turning after the church which leads to the graveyard entrance.

Saint Paul's of Rusland was built in 1745 of local undressed stone. It has an elevated position overlooking the tranquil Rusland valley. Arthur Ransome had his ashes buried in the graveyard, overlooking a landscape which he considered to be the finest in Britain.

✦ Continue along the lane, keeping left after the church, passing between farm buildings and leading to a crossroads. Turn left here, leading uphill quite steeply. In just under a mile bear right, signposted 'Hawkshead 4$^1/_2$ miles'.

The road crosses Dale Park Beck via Low Dale Park Bridge. (Cumbrians seem very keen on putting names on their bridges, which is quite convenient if you happen to have lost your way). Quarter of a mile after the bridge is a picnic area on the left, with a footpath leading off into the forest. This is the south-east corner of Grizedale Forest, famed for its forest trails and wood sculptures. The road follows the course of the Dale Park Beck keeping the forest on the left and mixed woodland on the right. It is a quiet, unspoilt, sheltered valley, along which there are three small groups of dwellings, called respectively Low, Middle and High Dale Park.

✦ After High Dale Park the road crosses the beck again and begins to rise, becoming quite steep, at which point, unless you have got a decent speed up it may be necessary to walk. The road twists into the trees and has many false horizons: it levels for a short way, allowing you to think you've reached the top, then it begins to climb again. The good news however, is that this is the last upward stretch and it's downhill practically all the way back to Hawkshead. After the climb the road drops steadily down towards Esthwaite Water. Bear left at the bottom and enjoy the final two miles. At the village turn left onto the B-road and left again for the car park. Secure your bike to the railings by the phone box and go in search of a cafe. 'A Room with a View', above a gift shop in the centre of the village is highly recommended.

CONISTON TO GRIZEDALE

RUSKIN, RANSOME &
THE SCULPTURES IN THE FOREST

Starting Points: either the lakeside car park, Coniston (SD308972); or, main car park, Tilberthwaite Avenue, Coniston (SD303976); or, Monk Coniston car park, near head of lake (SD316978).

Distance: 26 to 30 miles, depending on starting point and return route.

Terrain: Roads, with a few climbs. Optional return on forest trackways or via roads..

Time: $3^1/_2$ hours.

Maps: OS Landranger 97; OS Touring Map 3.

Public Toilets: Coniston, Monk Coniston car park; Brantwood, toilets for patrons only; Grizedale Visitor Centre; Hawkshead, near car park

Refreshments: Coniston: cafés, restaurants, pubs; Brantwood: tearoom; Oxen Park: 'The Manor House', pub; Satterthwaite: 'Eagle's Head', pub; Grizedale Forest: tearoom, restaurant; Hawkshead: cafés, restaurants, pubs.

This route takes in Brantwood, the home of John Ruskin, and includes a gentle ride along the eastern shore of Coniston Water. The return journey passes through Grizedale Forest with its fascinating sculptures set amongst the trees. Most of the route is mildly undulating and easily manageable, though there are a few longer uphill stretches. The choice of starting point allows you to either spend time in Coniston itself, avoid it altogether, or take the Ruskin launch across the lake to the Monk Coniston car park or Brantwood. The cost for cycle and rider is nominal.

✦ From the lakeside via launch:the lakeside car park can be found by following the 'P' signs along Lake Road. From the pier here the motor launch *Ruskin* crosses the lake to Monk Coniston, making regular trips throughout the season (check at tourist information centre for times out of season).

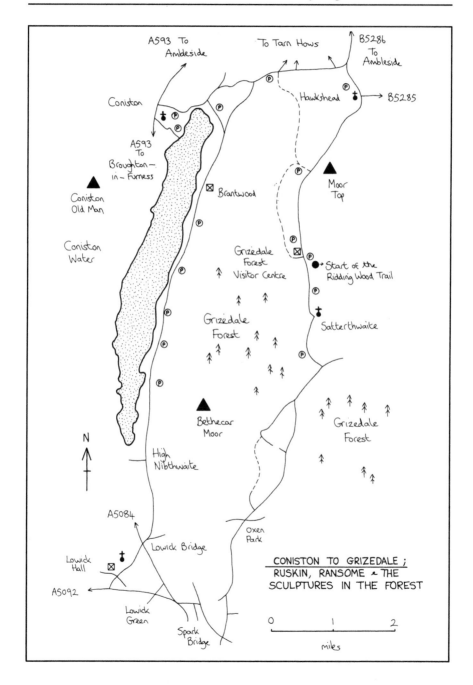

A593 To
Ambleside

To Tarn Hows

B5286
To
Ambleside

Coniston

Ⓟ

Hawkshead

Ⓟ

B5285

A593
To
Broughton—
in—Furness

Ⓟ

Ⓟ

▲
Coniston
Old Man

⊠ Brantwood

Ⓟ

▲
Moor
Top

Coniston
Water

Ⓟ

Ⓟ

⊠

Ⓟ

Grizedale
Forest
Visitor Centre

● Start of the
Ridding Wood Trail

Ⓟ

Ⓟ

Satterthwaite

Ⓟ

Grizedale
Forest

Ⓟ

Ⓟ

▲
Bethecar
Moor

Grizedale
Forest

N
↑

High
Nibthwaite

A5084

Oxen
Park

Lowick Bridge

⊠
Lowick
Hall

**CONISTON TO GRIZEDALE ;
RUSKIN, RANSOME & THE
SCULPTURES IN THE FOREST**

A5092

Lowick
Green

Spark
Bridge

0   1   2

miles

✦ From the central car park: bear right onto the road (B5285, heading in the Hawkshead direction) and follow the road out of the village. This meets the water's edge for a quarter of a mile, after which take the first right turning around the head of the lake. Monk Coniston car park is on the right, where there are toilets.

Coniston (meaning 'the king's farm') is a bustling village. There are numerous cafés, tearooms, restaurants and pubs, and no shortage of gift shops. The church of Saint Andrew in the village centre boasts the grave of John Ruskin. The headstone is of stone quarried from nearby Tilberthwaite, carved by local craftsmen into a tall Celtic cross, decorated with intricate designs relating to Ruskin's life and works. Also in the town is the Ruskin Museum (on Yewdale Road, almost opposite the Tourist Information centre) an essential port of call for any Ruskin disciple.

✦ From Monk Coniston car park:bear right onto the lane and follow the road as it climbs around 'Tent Lodge'. continue on to Brantwood (just over 1 mile).

The road undulates quite mildly, tree-lined on the left, giving good views to the right over the lake back towards Coniston. Dominating the view, towering high above the village is the 'Old Man', a rocky fell littered with mining remains: disused shafts and quarrying scars. It is 801 metres above sea level and from the summit cairn there are views of the surrounding fells and valleys, as far as Morecambe Bay in the south.

It was on Coniston water that Donald Campbell was killed in 1967 while attempting to break the Water speed record. His craft *Bluebird* flipped over at 300 mph and exploded. His body and the bulk of the wreckage were never found.

Also on the lake is the National Trust's renovated steam yacht *Gondola*, originally built in 1859. Now restored to its former glory it makes trips along the lake calling at Brantwood and Park-a-Moor, further down the eastern shore.

Brantwood was the home of John Ruskin, who lived here for the last 28 years of his life. Ruskin was an artist, but it was as a writer (with dozens of books to his name) and critic that he became famous and changed the face of art. He also became known for his work as a social campaigner and reformer. He was appalled by the poverty in the industrial towns of the north and proposed free schooling, minimum wages and rent control, none of which actually came about in his lifetime. Gandhi, Proust and Tolstoy were all influenced by him. To put it in a nutshell, Ruskin was a talented and thoroughly decent chap.

Coniston Water and 'The Old Man' from Brantwood

He bought Brantwood for £1,500 without ever having seen it, feeling that any house in such a setting could not fail to be worth the money. The house was small and unimpressive then, but Ruskin added to it considerably, including a 'turret' tacked onto the corner of his bedroom, so he had panoramic views over the lake to the opposite shore and 'The Old Man'. In the last years of his life he suffered from depression and disillusionment, and would sit in the turret in his wheelchair looking out over the water. He died in 1900.

Brantwood means 'steep wood'; it is built on a steep, wooded slope and backs onto the forest at Grizedale. The house is open daily from March to November (Wed-Sun in winter months) and is filled with Ruskin's sketches and watercolours. There is a fascinating video show (lasting about 20 minutes): an insight into the life and work of the great man. There is a good bookshop, selling books by/about Ruskin and other subjects of Lakeland interest. Also within the ground is a craft-shop, gallery, walks through the woods behind the house, toilets and the 'Jumping Jenny' tearoom and restaurant, named after Ruskin's boat. You don't have to pay the entry fee to the house to make use of the tearoom either. In nice weather you can sit out on the terrace and admire the views that so impressed Ruskin, AND your coffee cup will be refilled when empty.

✦ From Brantwood turn left and continue along the lakeside road, heading south.

This road along the eastern shore is excellent for cycling. It winds frequently, but never too tightly, and its hills are only minor. There are good views across the lake for most of the way and access to the water's edge at several points towards the middle and lower reaches. On the left are dense woodlands, mainly National Trust owned, and the thick forests which are the western edge of Grizedale.

On the left, 1.5 miles after Brantwood, is 'The Heald', a long cottage of grey local stone. From 1940-45 this was the home of Arthur Ransome, author of 'Swallows and Amazons' and a string of other best-selling childrens' classics. He described it as a place he had been "a bit in love with since the age of nine" and said that its views over the lake towards the Coniston Old Man were "better even than Brantwood".

Ransome loved to sail on the lake and picnicked on Peel Island with friends (visible towards the bottom of the lake) where he also corrected proofs of his work. This craggy, tree-covered island was the main inspiration for the 'Wild Cat Island' from his stories.

As the road leaves the bottom of the lake it passes through High Nibthwaite, a pretty village of whitewashed stone, following the course of the Coniston Water outflow, the River Crake. As a boy, Ransome and his parents spent many summers staying on a farm here, when he first grew to know and love the area.

✦ 3 miles after High Nibthwaite the road ends at a T-junction. Bear right across Lowick Bridge, then cross the main road into Lowick.

On the right in the village of Lowick is the Red Lion (with a beer garden), where Arthur Ransome used to drink as a young man, after a long walk from his lodgings. Shortly after Lowick's white cottages the road rises slightly to Saint Luke's, a small church on the right, after which is the driveway to Lowick Hall (the house itself is hidden in the trees) which Ransome and his Russian wife bought in later life. He wrote none of his childrens' fiction here, but did work extensively on his autobiography. The hall needed a great deal of serious restoration and general maintenance, and after two years the Ransomes were forced to sell it at a loss.

✦ Take the next left turning down a narrow lane, which rises slightly. Turn left at the T-junction (onto the A5092) passing the school on the left. Turn left by the Farmers Arms and descend into Spark Bridge.

The bridge in question crosses the River Crake, which effectively cuts the village in half. On the left is the Royal Oak.

✦ Cross the bridge and follow the road which climbs not too steeply, but it is a slow drag. In just under 1 mile is a crossroads. Turn left, signposted 'Oxen Park & Hawkshead'.

This is very pleasant countryside, well away from the tourist hotspots. The lanes are quiet, with grassy banks and hawthorn hedges. The villages in this area are quaint enough, but they are practical; in no way are they postcard villages. There are very few amenities for the traveller. Even pubs are few and far between. Riding around here in the early evening you would probably not meet anyone, and the silence of the landscape is almost unbelievable. This is what it sounded like a hundred years ago.

After a welcome downhill stretch the road crosses a stream and the land opens out on the left, giving good views of fields, forest and the Coniston fells in the distance.

✦ Follow the lane through the hamlet of Colton and make the last short climb to Oxen Park.

Oxen Park is a small village built around a confluence of roads. It is quite high up and catches the wind on a breezy day. Some of the older cottages amidst the tight cluster of dwellings are 16th century. On the left is the friendly village pub, The Manor House: a suitable place to stop for a celebratory drink, as Oxen Park marks the last of the serious uphill climbs. It also has seats outside, so on a fine day you can sit in the sunshine and admire your bike.

✦ From Oxen Park continue along the main village street, ignoring the various turnings on either side. Follow the road downhill to Force Forge.

Anyone with a mountain bike might like to make use of the drive on the left, used as a bridleway. It starts off as a firm, if grass encroached, trackway, but soon lapses into a rough gravel path. Where it rejoins the lane keep bearing left into Satterthwaite. The best route though is to stick to the road, which drops steadily for two miles. As the road levels, notice on the right, in the centre of a field a lone standing stone, a relic from prehistory.

✦ Continue past Rook How (18th century Quaker meeting house on the left) and follow the road through the hamlet of Force Forge. A mile later you will come to its sister hamlet, Force Mills, after which bear left into Grizedale Forest.

Force Forge is a minute community of cottages and farm buildings, and is so called because there was once a water powered iron forge there. The road follows the course of Force Beck and crosses it via Force Mill Bridge. Around the corner is a sign announcing the beginning of Grizedale Forest, the logo of which incorporates a pig or boar, as Grizedale means, predictably enough, 'the dale of the pig' in Norse. On the immediate left you will find Force Falls and a woodland pathway, part of Grizedale's 9.5 mile 'Silurian Trail', waymarked by green posts. Close to the beck you should see the first of the famous forest sculptures, many made out of waste forest materials such as fallen boughs and brushwood. This one is entitled 'Her Insistent Stream'.

Wood sculptures, Grizedale Forest

The sculptures are scattered throughout the forest and it would take you a full day to see them all. There are guides and location maps available from the Visitor Centre further along the route. Sculptures are occasionally removed, relocated or replaced, so if you can't find one it probably means it isn't there any more – but do not despair, there are plenty of others.

✦ Follow the road into Satterthwaite (just over a mile).

On the right, clearly visible from the road, is another sculpture, on the edge of a school playing field: 'Heron and Swan'. After the field the road crosses the beck, at which point there is a picnic site.

Satterthwaite is set in the midst of the forest and was originally a Norse farm holding. Norse invaders settled throughout the area and left a legacy of Scandinavian place names. Satterthwaite means 'the summer farm in the clearing'. Little is ever written about it in guidebooks, as there is very little here to please the tourist. The Eagle's Head pub is on the left towards the beginning of the village. It serves food and has a small beer garden. The church of All Saints with its lychgate and crenellated tower stands to the right of the road in the centre of the village.

✦ From Satterthwaite follow the road a further two miles past the campsite on the right, into Grizedale itself. The visitor centre is on the left, which is a suitable place to chain your bike.

Grizedale is the heart of the forest. Close to the Visitor Centre there are toilets, cafeteria, the 'Gallery in the Forest' with exhibitions and displays regarding the forest sculptures, and an excellent gift shop selling maps and guides of the forest, including cycling routes, sculpture trails and orienteering courses. Next to the cafeteria is the booking office for the intimate 'Theatre in the Forest', which gives evening performances and attracts international stars.

There are miles of paths through the forest, but if you just want a short walk then the Ridding Wood Trail is the best and is packed with sculptures. It starts from the car park on the opposite side of the road, next to the campsite. Of particular interest are the amusing attractions such as the 'Squirrel Marimba' and 'Oak Xylophone'. The trail should take about half an hour in all.

If you want to return to Coniston via the forest road network there are various routes that are open to cycles. A cheap map can be purchased from the Visitor Centre shop, showing all the forest roads available. (For the most direct route follow first the blue then the red cycles. This is also included on the Coniston to Grizedale route map, starting from the Visitor Centre or Moor Top.)

✦ From the visitor centre turn left back onto the lane. Follow the road, which climbs at first, but is mainly downhill all the way. Take care on the final descent between the cottages as the road is steep and winds considerably. Turn left at the bottom for Hawkshead (half a mile) turn left onto the B-road which skirts the village, and if you want to stop here turn left again for the car park.

Hawkshead is one of the most popular tourist villages, typical picture postcard stuff. It was here that young William Wordsworth did his schooling, at the grammar next to the church, now open to the public. The church itself is worth a visit, if only to take in the view from its graveyard of the village and surrounding countryside. The village is also the home of the National Trust's Beatrix Potter Gallery, housed in what was her solicitor husband's offices. There are various picture galleries and craft shops, a good Tourist Information Centre with free displays, numerous cafés and inns. Unfortunately, it always seems to be over-crowded in Hawkshead, particularly at week-ends.

✦ From Hawkshead follow the B-road around the village and after the houses bear left along the B5285, signed for Coniston: the beginning of a long, slow climb.

A glance back over your shoulder will give good views of the Central Fells towards Ambleside: High Pike, Fairfield and also the attractive pastures around Hawkshead. If you're ultra-fit with a fantastic bike, you might like to tackle the steep lanes to the right and head for the renowned beauty-spot of Tarn Hows. There are numerous signs pointing the way and all roads from here seem to lead there. It is a much visited, much-photographed place, appearing on hundreds of postcards and practically every Lakeland calendar. It deserves its reputation but be warned, it is uphill all the way. Once there you can continue along the road past the National Trust car park, which drops down to the Coniston road. The best time to visit 'the Tarns' is early morning or late afternoon, while all the motoring visitors are having their breakfast or tea.

✦ After the climb up from Hawkshead the road levels and soon begins to descend steeply towards Coniston Water.

On the left there is an unusual commemorative well, built in 1885. As well as a dried up drinking fountain there is a water-filled trough for horses, above which it reads: 'A righteous man regardeth the life of his beast'. It isn't advisable to actually drink any, as it is probably full of floating cigarette ends.

✦ Follow the road downhill, with woodland on both sides. The road bends around Monk Coniston Hall on the left and arrives at the water's edge. Bear left for the Monk Coniston car park. Continue ahead for Coniston village and the central and lakeside car parks.

The North and North-Western Lakes

DERWENT WATER

THE 'QUEEN OF THE LAKES'

Starting point: Central car park, Keswick (NY265234)

Distance: 11 miles.

Terrain: Good roads, mainly flat; no serious climbs.

Time: 1$^1/_2$ hours

Maps: OS Outdoor Leisure 4; OS Landranger 90; OS Touring Map 3.

Public Toilets: Keswick town centre; Grange in Borrowdale

Refreshments: Keswick: restaurants, cafés, pubs, take-aways; Grange: tearooms; Lingholm Gardens: tearoom

Derwent Water is known as the 'Queen of the Lakes', though there is a strong body of opinion that believes the title should belong to Ullswater. The lake is much quieter than Windermere, having few powered craft on its water. It is the widest of the sixteen lakes, being 1$^1/_4$ miles across, but only 72 feet at its deepest. It is surrounded by some spectacular scenery and the view from the north of the lake towards Borrowdale is one of the most popular and easily recognised views in Lakeland. There is a regular ferry service (not suitable for cycles) stopping at various convenient points around the lake, and well worth a trip, if only for the views.

✦ Leave Keswick's central car park, turning left. After a few hundred yards there is a small roundabout; take the first exit, signed to Borrowdale.

The second exit at the roundabout leads to another car park and the lakeside, where there are toilets and several tea rooms (with outside seats available). It is from this point that the ferries depart and rowing boats are available for hire. There are walks along the shore to the well-known beauty spot and view point, Friar's Crag.

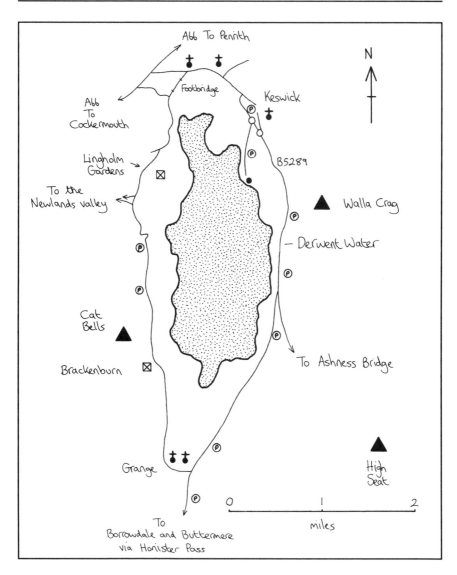

◆ At the second roundabout take the last exit, again signed for Borrowdale.

If you are interested in churches (or specifically Hugh Walpole's grave) make a detour along the first exit and take the footpath off to the right for Saint John's Church, built of sandstone in 1838. The elegant spire, quite rare in the Lakes, can easily be picked out amidst the grey rooftops from any of the surrounding fells that overlook the town.

The Borrowdale road runs all the way along the eastern shore of Derwent Water. On the left there are mixed woodlands, and above them the rocky face of Walla Crag. On the right there are several footpaths, all leading to the water's edge.

Half way down the lake there is a turning to the left, which climbs steadily to the much photographed Ashness Bridge (which can be found on every Lakeland calendar and scores of postcards) a pack horse bridge which spans the powerful mountain waters of Watendlath Beck, on its way to the lake. From the bridge there are good views of the Skiddaw range to the north of Keswick. If you do decide to make a detour to Ashness, return the same way back to the Borrowdale road.

✦ 1 mile after the end of the lake take the right turning across the River Derwent into Grange.

The double-arched bridge at Grange is quite famous; another pack-horse bridge built in the 17th century to span the Derwent on its way into Derwent Water. Grange was once owned by the monks of Furness Abbey, who had one of their granaries here (Grange means 'granary'). Today Grange is a tiny community surrounded by high rocky crags. It has a couple of chapels and a couple of cafés for the tourists who pass through. There are toilets on the left, look for the sign above the post box.

Just after the village are several footpaths leading up to High Spy, the highest fell on the left, with extensive views, especially to the south.

The road climbs slightly to Low Manesty, after which it enters National Trust woodlands. Footpaths to the right lead to the shore of Derwent Water. Look out for 'Brackenburn' on the left, the home of novelist Hugh Walpole from 1923, until his death, though he never stayed here for more than five weeks without returning to London. He wrote many of his novels here, including the 'Herries' sagas, all set in the locality. The house is built of grey Lakeland stone and there is a small round plaque on the front in memory of the author. The garage doors are still blue, as they were in Walpole's day. The bay window over the garage doors was his library and study, where he could sit and look out at the unspoilt view over the lake.

Walpole died in 1941 and was buried at Saint John's Church in

Keswick in a spot he had chosen for himself. A grey Celtic cross marks his grave, bearing the words 'Man of letters. Lover of Cumberland.' The red sandstone spire of the church can be seen from Cat Bells, the fell behind the house, on which there is a commemorative seat marking one of Walpole's favourite spots, placed there by Harold Cheevers, who was the author's friend and chauffeur, who lived with him. To climb Cat Bells take the footpath half a mile after Brackenburn, bearing left along a gently climbing footpath which does get steeper and involves a few scrambles over bare rock on the last climb to the summit. There are good views over Derwent Water to Bassenthwaite Lake beyond, over Keswick to the Skiddaw range in the background. To the west there are views down into the Newlands valley and the high fells beyond. If you only climb one fell in the area, make sure it is Cat Bells.

Shortly after the footpath is the National Trust woodland, Brandelhow Park, which was the first property acquired by the Trust in 1902, through which there are footpaths down to the lake, and excellent walking along the shore, where there are several shingle bays and rocky peninsulas.

✦ Follow the road along the lower slopes of Cat Bells. Beware of the sharp bend to the right as the road steeply descends and crosses a cattle grid. Continue into an area of evergreen forest. Keswick is signposted 3 miles.

Notice on the right the driveway to Lingholm Gardens, open in summer from 10 to 5. The Victorian house (not open to the public) has had several famous visitors, including Beatrix Potter, who spent many summer holidays here and made several sketches which were later incorporated in her books. The gardens are best seen in late spring/early summer. There are footpaths to the shore and a tearoom.

✦ Follow the road to the right at the next junction, signed 'Keswick 1³/₄ miles'. In the village of Portinscale turn right (with the post office on the left). The road drops down past the Derwent Water Hotel to a narrow footbridge over the river Derwent, on its way to Bassenthwaite Lake. There is a sign forbidding cycling on the bridge, so make sure you walk across, then follow the lane and bear right for Keswick town centre.

The main road passes the Pencil Museum, which boasts the largest pencil in the world and proudly claims to be the 'home of the world's first pencils'.

For the Keswick Museum and Art Gallery follow the main road through the town centre and bear left for Fitz Park. The exhibits include the diaries of Hugh Walpole and various letters and documents relating to the Lake Poets, as well as the renowned musical stones, quarried from Skiddaw in the 1800s.

✦ To return to the central car park (from the Pencil Museum) take the next main right turning past the bus station and follow the road round, then bear left into the car park.

Ferry landing on the western shore of Derwent Water, with Blencathra and the Skiddaw range in the background

KESWICK, LORTON AND BASSENTHWAITE

VIA WHINLATTER AND WYTHOP

Starting point: Central car park, Keswick (NY265234).

Distance: 25 miles.

Terrain: Good roads, short distances on A roads. No off-road cycling. Steep climb towards Whinlatter Pass, but otherwise relatively flat.

Maps: OS Landranger 90; OS Outdoor Leisure 4.

Public toilets: Keswick; Whinlatter Visitor Centre; Dodd Wood car park, off A591.

Refreshments: Keswick: cafés, pubs, restaurants; Whinlatter Visitor Centre: café & take-away snacks; Wythop Mill: Water Mill café/restaurant; Various pubs around northern end of Bassenthwaite Lake; Old Saw Mill (tearoom) Dodd Wood.

Apart from the climb up to the Whinlatter Pass, this route has no severe gradients. The countryside is quite varied, including forested areas, the pleasant pastures of the Lorton valley, quiet villages and good views of Skiddaw and Bassenthwaite Lake. Allow plenty of time for the Whinlatter Visitor Centre. Make sure you allow time for the café as well.

Cycling is permitted in the forest itself. For route guidance and advice ask at the information desk in the shop.

✦ From Keswick's central car park turn right onto the road, then left at the T-junction. Either continue to the A.66 (1 mile) and bear left heading for Braithwaite (1 mile) or, for a less direct, but more picturesque route avoiding the main road, bear left off the B5289 and cross the footbridge (walking!). Continue up the hill past the Derwent Water Hotel into Portinscale. Turn left and follow the road into a wooded area, taking the first right around the lower slopes of Swinside Fell towards Ullock. Bear right and pass through Little Braithwaite next to Newlands Beck. Bear right again for Braithwaite. In the village turn left onto the B5292 and follow signs for the Whinlatter Pass.

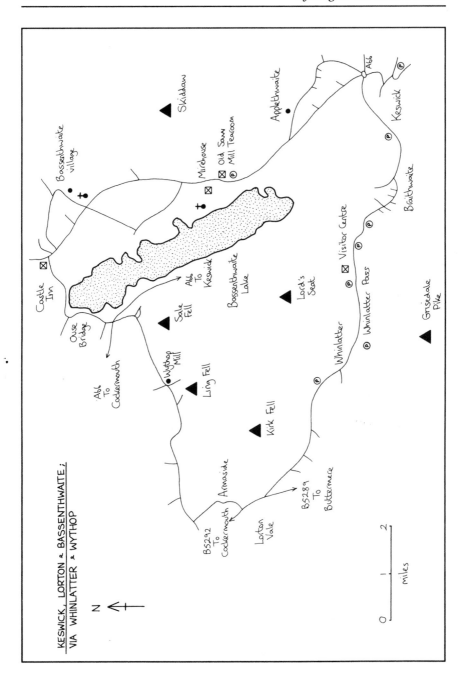

KESWICK, LORTON & BASSENTHWAITE:
VIA WHINLATTER & WYTHOP

Braithwaite has an old village centre, but has been ruined by new prefabricated houses. On the whole it carries the overspill from Keswick. The B-road passing through it is very narrow in parts and winds continually until it enters the edge of the Thornthwaite Forest, at which point it begins to rise quite steeply. After 1 mile there is a viewpoint on the right at a small lay-by, looking out over the edge of the forest to Bassenthwaite Lake and Skiddaw. The approach to the viewpoint is the most severe stretch, after which the road levels out somewhat. The Whinlatter Visitor Centre on the right marks the end of the uphill struggle. It is well worth a visit as there is plenty to do here. The cafe is pleasant and has a take-away service with picnic tables outside. There is a well stocked shop selling gifts, maps and books, and also leaflets and nature trail guides on the surrounding area. You might like to try your hand at Orienteering, and there are specially designed trails for children. There is a free audio visual show giving a brief history of the forest and pass, and animated displays relating to forestry and timber production. There are miles of footpaths and forest tracks to explore, many leading up to higher ground such as Seat How with its view over the Vale of Keswick. The forest is a fascinating place and deserves at least a few hours of your day.

◆ From the visitor centre turn right and head downhill towards the Vale of Lorton (4 miles).

On the right the trees end and there is an open fellside of loose rock and heather. This is Whinlatter, the fell from which the pass takes its name. On the left there are more forest walks on the lower slopes of Grisedale Pike, probably the most climbed peak in the immediate area.

◆ Follow the road, taking care on the tight downhill bends (1:8) with Blaze Beck on the left in its tree-lined ravine. Join the Lorton Vale road, bearing right, signed 'Cockermouth 3$^1/_4$'.

Lorton Vale is a green, fertile valley, through which flows the River Cocker on its way to Cockermouth. The surrounding fells are low and rounded, uncharacteristic of the Lake District, but there are views behind of the rocky giants such as Grasmoor, to remind you where you are.

◆ Take the first right (half a mile after the junction) along a narrow, single track lane, overgrown with grass in the middle. The road climbs very slightly between hawthorn hedges, winding past High Armaside (farm). Pass under the pylons then bear right at the T-junction.

Ahead is an area of green pastures, very quiet, very rural, with little intrusion by the holiday-maker. Again there are views to the right of the high fells along the Buttermere valley.

✦ Follow the road again under the pylons, heading east to the hamlet of Wythop mill.

On the left after the pylons is the little church of Saint Cuthbert's, rebuilt in 1806, which has a graveyard of crooked, lichen-encrusted stones and a minute bell tower with its two bells visible.

The road winds downhill after the church, then gradually upwards, skirting the edge of Ling Fell, then down again into Wythop (pronounced 'Withup') Mill, a small village taking its name from a 19th century water-powered sawmill (off to the left, look for the sign: 'Mill 30 yards') now fully restored and open as a museum (April to October, daily except Monday. Weekends only in winter). There is a café/restaurant attached with 'healthy options' choice of food.

✦ Pass straight through Wythop mill village, over Wythop Beck, continuing uphill with Sale Fell on the right.

The road crosses the lower slopes of Sale Fell, covered with gorse and ferns. 1 mile after Wythop Mill village is the Church of Saint Margaret with its lofty weathercock, built to replace an earlier building high up on Sale Fell, now in ruins. Shortly after Saint Margaret's, Bassenthwaite Lake comes into view on the left.

✦ Continue downhill towards the lake. Bear left at the junction, signed for Cockermouth. Cross the A66 and take the lane signed for 'Castle Inn'. Take the first right, again signed for Castle Inn.

This road passes close to the northern tip of Bassenthwaite Lake and there are glimpses of the water through the trees. Close to Ouse Bridge there are parking lay-bys with steps down to the shore-line, offering views along the length of the lake and of the Skiddaw range to the east.

✦ Bear right over the red stone Ouse Bridge which crosses the River Derwent. Continue along the road to Castle Inn (1.25 miles).

Looking across Bassenthwaite Lake towards Whinlatter Forest Park

This is a sheltered, leafy lane. On the left is the entrance to Armathwaite Hall, now an exclusive hotel, once the home of the wealthy Spedding family, who later moved around the lake to Mirehouse. The hotel was featured on ITV's 'Blind Date' as the location for a young couple to see how much they didn't like each other (they didn't end up getting married).

The Castle Inn stands at the end of the road at a junction with the A591. The building is several hundred years old, much altered and now a popular drive-to pub and restaurant.

✦ Turn right onto the A591, then take the second left signed for Bassenthwaite village. After 1 mile turn right over a bridge into the village itself.

As with many Cumbrian towns and villages, Bassenthwaite village is actually over a mile from the lake of the same name. The Sun Inn is on the right after the bridge. It was here that Keats, on a Lakeland tour, took a break after climbing Skiddaw.

✦ Turn left after the village green, then straight across at the crossroads along a flat and narrow lane, shadowed by overhanging branches. At the T-junction (just under 1 mile) turn left, signposted for Keswick. There is a short climb to the main road. Bear right.

In just under a mile on the right is Mirehouse, the home of the Spedding family, built in 1666. The grounds are open daily throughout the season (Easter to October) but the house is only open Wednesdays, Sundays and Bank Holidays, from 2 to 5 pm. Just over the road is Dodd Wood, where you will find the Old Sawmill Tearooms (open daily) and public toilets. There are various footpaths through the woods leading uphill, giving good views over the lake if you get high enough and continuing up to Skiddaw.

✦ Take the next left turning with the plantations of Dodd Wood on the left. Continue through Millbeck and Applethwaite. Bear left, heading downhill opposite the Applethwaite Country House Hotel (just over 1.5 miles). Follow the road down to the roundabout (1 mile) and take the second exit for Keswick town centre. Take care, this stretch of road is busy, but unavoidable. Turn left at the junction and left again by the telephone boxes. Follow the road round to the car park on the left.

KESWICK TO BUTTERMERE

VIA THE PASSES

Starting point: Central Car Park, Keswick (NY265234)

Distance: 30 miles

Terrain: Good roads, a few fairly steep climbs, two severely steep.

Time: 5 hours if you push yourself, but better to allow a full day.

Maps: OS Outdoor Leisure 4; OS Touring map 3

Public Toilets: Keswick town centre; Whinlatter Visitor Centre, Whinlatter Pass; Buttermere village; Seatoller village; Car park, Borrowdale (near Bowder Stone)

Refreshments: Keswick: cafés, restaurants, pubs, take-away food; Whinlatter Visitor Centre: café, take-away drinks/snacks; Buttermere: cafés, licensed hotels; Borrowdale: craft shop/tearoom, on left just before turning for Grange.

This route is not for those without stamina or strong legs. There are two main uphill stretches, those being the steep approaches to the Whinlatter and Honister Passes. They are both quite severe (but particularly the latter) and you will almost certainly have to walk at least some of the way up. That said, the majority of the rest of the circuit is relatively flat and there are some long and very welcome downhill runs. The scenery (as always) is spectacular.

✦ From Keswick's central car park turn right, then left at the T-junction (with the telephone boxes on the right corner) bearing in a westerly direction. In 1 mile the road joins the A66. Bear left towards Braithwaite and left again in another mile, cutting through Braithwaite village and heading for the Whinlatter Pass.

Braithwaite is a mixture of old painted stone houses and new, grey prefabs. It is definitely not a picture postcard village. The B-road through its centre can be difficult to follow, becoming very narrow in places and winding sharply between buildings. Fortunately, the Whinlatter Pass is signposted frequently

✦ Pass the Royal Oak on the left, shortly after which the road begins to climb quite steeply, getting steeper. After the lay-by on the right it becomes less severe.

The lay-by is marked on Ordnance Survey maps as a viewpoint and gives views of the Thornthwaite Forest and towards Bassenthwaite Lake and the Skiddaw range, which dominates most views in the area.

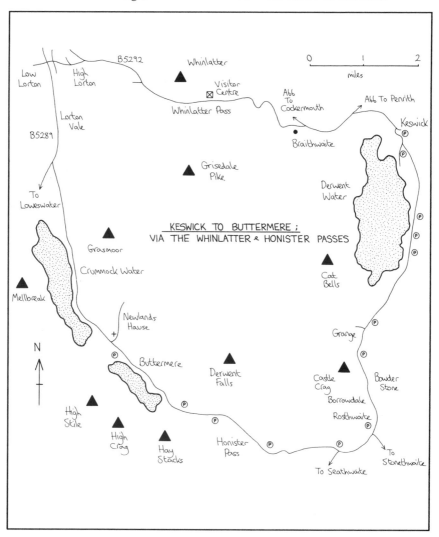

KESWICK TO BUTTERMERE ;
VIA THE WHINLATTER & HONISTER PASSES

The forest on the left of the road is known as the 'Hospital Plantation', as there was once a hospital there for sailors who were suffering from illnesses such as TB, so they could be kept in isolation.

When you pass the Cottage in the Wood hotel and restaurant you're almost at the top of the hill. On the right in less than a quarter of a mile is the Whinlatter Visitor Centre and Forest Park. The latter was opened by Chris Bonington on 3rd September 1993. I missed him by one day! It is well worth stopping to make use of the facilities, such as the toilets if nothing else. There is an attractive restaurant/tearoom which looks out over the trees, and also a hatch serving take-away snacks and drinks, with tables outside. There is a well stocked gift shop, free visual presentation about the history of the forest as well as an imaginative and high-tech display about trees and timber production, not forgetting the walk-through reconstruction of a badger sett.

There are various trails through the forest, including two specifically for children, the 'Fox Trot' and 'Rabbit Run', also there are nature trails, a puzzle trail, orienteering, mountain bike hire . . . definitely a place to spend a least a couple of hours. The centre and amenities are open daily 10am to 5.30pm.

✦ From the visitor centre turn right onto the road, which drops gently downhill.

On the right the trees end and for a mile there is an open fellside of loose rock and heather. This is Whinlatter, the fell from which the pass takes its name. Running parallel to the road on the left, but hidden in the trees for most of the way is Whinlatter Gill.

✦ Avoid the first left turn to Lorton. There are now grassy slopes on the left and a plantation on the right. Beware of the tight downhill bends (1:8) with Blaze Beck rushing on the left in its tree-lined ravine. Take the next left (1 mile) down a single track lane, signed 'unfit for heavy traffic'. This drops down to High Lorton and comes out at a T-junction between Corner House and Corner Cottage. Turn left and follow the road past the post office on the left. Straight ahead at the small cross roads to Low Lorton, then turn left onto the B5289.

This is Lorton Vale, pleasantly green, through which flows the River Cocker, on its way to Cockermouth just a few miles to the north. Low Lorton is made up of pleasant white cottages. You may notice a turret rising from the stone wall opposite. This is part of Lorton Hall, privately owned and not open to the public. There is a pub at the other end of the village, the Wheatsheaf Inn, which will mean double-backing for a quarter of a mile. Lorton was immortalised by Wordsworth, who wrote in his poem 'Yew Trees': 'a yew tree, pride of Lorton Vale, which to this day stands single, in the midst of its own darkness'. The tree in question, now long gone, stood behind the village hall, called, not surprisingly, Yew Tree Hall.

✦ 2 miles after Low Lorton, bear left towards Crummock Water.

After a few initial climbs the road is relatively flat with a few good downhill stretches. After the cattle grid (just over a mile from the junction) there are good views over the lake towards Mellbreak (fell) opposite. At this point there is a path to the left which heads up to the rocky peak of Grasmoor, the giant of the region (852 metres – 2791 feet – above sea level). From the summit you can see practically everything, including the Scafells, Helvellyn, Skiddaw, the Langdale Pikes, Fairfield, and every other fell and mountain worth its salt.

On the right of the road is a footpath leading down through the National Trust's Lanthwaite Woods to the water's edge. Crummock is Celtic, meaning 'crooked', ie: 'Crooked Lake'. It is now owned by the National Trust and is usually fairly quiet, attracting far fewer visitors that Buttermere, which is just next door. The two neighbouring lakes were once one large lake, though now there is a band of land between them. The imposing fell on the opposite side of Crummock Water is Mellbreak, covered with heather and scree. As Wainwright says: "a grand hill in a beautiful situation. There is only one Mellbreak."

Also on the opposite slopes is Scale Force, a waterfall with the longest drop in the Lake District. Guidebooks give various drastically differing measurements, from 120 to 200 feet. You'll have to make up your own mind. It can be reached by a cobbled lane leading past the Fish Hotel in Buttermere. Mountain bikers (or any cyclist with good gears and brakes) can ride almost all the way there, along the public bridleways.

The road passes close to Crummock's shore at Hause Point, where there is access to a small shingle beach: a nice place to stop, throw in a few stones, admire the views and take a couple of photos.

✦ Continue along the road into Buttermere village (just under 3 miles).

Buttermere has pubs, hotels, cafés and many visitors, yet it is a small village – you could cycle through it in under a minute. The Bridge Hotel was originally a corn mill, and was licensed in 1735. It was at one time called the 'Queen Victoria', as the Queen once stayed here.

The Fish Inn is famous for being the home of Mary Robinson, the 'Beauty of Buttermere'. Mary was the inn-keeper's daughter, who was proposed to and subsequently married a man claiming to be an honourable gentleman and an MP, who turned out to be a con man with various wives and children scattered all over the country. When his sins were found out he was arrested for forgery and held in Carlisle awaiting his sentence, where the Wordsworths went to see him out of curiosity. The impostor was duly hanged in September 1803 and Mary returned to her family and bar work at the 'Fish', later marrying a farmer and moving to Caldbeck, north of Skiddaw. The story was fictionalized as 'The Maid of Buttermere' by Melvyn Bragg and became a best-seller.

Today, the centuries-old Fish Inn is not very impressive, having been marred by extensions at the rear and side. You pass it on the footpath to the far side of the lake: a fenced cobbled lane (and bridleway if you choose to cycle. The bridleway continues through the woods and alongside Buttermere, returning to the road at the end of the lake. Perhaps best left to the mountain bike brigade).

Towards the end of the lake on the far side, is a rocky fell with various rounded crags along its ridge. This is Haystacks, one of Wainwright's favourite fells: "a place of surprises around corners", he writes, "For beauty, variety . . . for sheer fascination . . . the summit area of Haystacks is supreme." Wainwright requested in his will that when he died his ashes would be scattered around Innominate Tarn (so called because it doesn't have a name) on Haystacks: "a quiet place; a lonely place". In accordance with his wishes, when he died in January 1991, his second wife carried his ashes up to his favourite fell and scattered them close to the tarn.

There are two paths (bridleways) leading (eventually) to the summit, from the hamlet of Gatesgarth, just after the end of the lake. The right hand path bears initially back towards Buttermere, then rises on the slopes of High Crag and via the Scarth Gap Pass to the Haystacks summit. The left hand path (just after the hamlet) crosses the lower slopes of Fleetwith Pike and by keeping right you should reach the summit via the Blackbeck and Innominate tarns.

Haystacks is dwarfed by the higher fells that surround it. At 597 metres it is no giant, but it is worth considering a visit because of its views over Buttermere and Crummock Water, and of Ennerdale over the other side, and because it is Wainwright's mountain.

✦ Back to the road, continuing south-east out of Buttermere.

On leaving the village you will pass the minute Church of Saint James, in which you will find an arched window with a view across the lake towards Haystacks. On the sill there is a grey slate commemorative plaque, which reads: 'Pause and Remember Alfred Wainwright . . . who loved this valley.'

Directly after the church is the road up to Newlands Hause, a pass between the mountains to Keswick, via the Newlands valley, but it is *very* steep from this side.

Along the Buttermere road there are good views across the lake, especially towards the southern tip, with the row of shore-line trees. It is an easy and pleasantly winding road, passing close to the water's edge before leaving the lake and heading to Gatesgarth, a popular parking place for those intending to scale the high fells that surround the area.

✦ Follow the open road which runs alongside Gatesgarthdale Beck, heading gradually up to the Honister Pass.

The ascent up to Honister is very gentle at first, along an unwalled road with steep slopes on each side. The heather gives way to thin grass, which in turn gives way to grey screes. On an overcast day everything here is grey. You can see the road ahead snaking up to the pass, and more often than not there will be a steady stream of vehicles moving along it. The lower fellsides are boulder-strewn, leading up to solid rock peaks.

Towards the end of the valley the gradient becomes severe, and it will almost certainly be necessary to walk and push your bike but, if taken at a leisurely pace with frequent stops to take a breath and admire the view, it is surprising how easy it is. After this climb it is downhill or flat all the way back to Keswick.

At the top of the Honister Pass there is a small car park, and the boarded up buildings of the Westmorland Green Slate Company, which recently closed down, next to which is the Honister Hause Youth Hostel.

✦ Follow the road on its winding descent into Borrowdale, dropping quite steeply through open marshland and marram grass. After $3/4$ mile cross the cattle grid, after which there is a sign: 'cyclists are strongly advised to walk'. If you do cycle down, go slowly and take the utmost care. Beware of oncoming traffic.

The road runs alongside Hause Gill into Seatoller, a village of 17th century slate cottages, built to house quarry workers and miners, who were employed on the surrounding fells, and who took to smuggling to supplement their incomes. There are public toilets and an information centre in a converted barn, which offers displays and talks. On the right is The Yew Tree, a restaurant with a beer garden, the building itself is of white-washed stone, and bears the date 1628 over the door.

As an optional detour (returning the same way) look out for the narrow turning to the right directly after the village, heading to Seathwaite (just over 1 mile) a small cluster of farm buildings wedged between mountains, reputed to have the highest rainfall in the whole of England. Once a prosperous mining area for graphite, which was needed for the construction of cannonballs and, of course, pencils. Graphite was much sought after and several fortunes were made. The Pencil Factory in Keswick opened in 1566, using Seathwaite graphite in its products.

✦ Continue into Borrowdale. Keswick is signed as 8 miles away.

Borrowdale, for hundreds of years, has been considered to be one of the most beautiful areas in the Lakes, especially by Wainwright, who saw it as "the loveliest and most precious valley in Lakeland. The road passes through Rosthwaite, where there is a general store on the right. From the car park (along the village back streets) there are footpaths leading into the woods alongside the River Derwent, and also up to Castle Crag, the lowest fell in the area (985 feet) but just about the best viewpoint for Borrowdale and Derwent Water. The Celtic tribe, the Brigantes, built a stronghold on the top, hence the name. Its lower slopes are wooded, but the trees thin out towards the summit of rough slate scree. Wainwright advises any visitor to the Lakes with just a few hours to spare to climb the fell.

Half a mile after Rosthwaite the road, undulating mildly, becomes surrounded by mixed trees. The river, running close on the left, is wide and clear: very picturesque. One of the reasons people visit Borrowdale is to see the famous Bowder Stone, which can be reached by a pathway on the right, just after a memorial well by the roadside. The huge boulder (36 feet high) is set in carefully managed National Trust wood-lands. It was left behind by a retreating glacier after the last Ice Age, balanced oddly in the woods, estimated to weigh 2,000 tons.

✦ Either bear left over the double bridge towards Grange for a more meandering route back to Keswick, or continue along the B-road that follows the eastern shore of Derwent Water. For a more detailed description of these two routes see the Derwent Water circular route. At the first roundabout on the approach to Keswick take the first exit. At the second roundabout take the second exit and continue into the town centre. The central car park is on the right.

Ferry landings on Derwent Water with the Skiddaw range in the background.

NEWLANDS

WAINWRIGHT'S 'SHY VALLEY'

Starting point: Portinscale village. 1 mile west of Keswick (NY251236) or Central Car Park, Keswick (NY265234).

Distance: Short circular route: 10 miles; Keswick to Buttermere: 9 miles.

Terrain: Circular route: narrow lanes, mainly quiet, mostly quite flat. No off-road cycling. To Buttermere: rises steadily towards the Newlands Hause, then climbs for a short way very steeply. No off-road cycling.

Maps: OS Landranger 90; OS Outdoor Leisure 4; OS Touring Map 3.

Public Toilets: Keswick and Buttermere.

Refreshments: Keswick: pubs, cafés, restaurants; Buttermere: cafés, hotels with public bars.

Wainwright regarded the Newlands Valley very highly. A "shy valley" because it is hidden from the main road that runs between Keswick and Cockermouth. If you didn't know it was there you would drive past none the wiser. Considering it is on Keswick's doorstep, it is surprisingly quiet and very picturesque.

This short circular route makes an excellent ride if you've only got an hour or two to spare. For a longer trip it can conveniently be tacked onto the Derwent Water circuit and can be used as a direct route to Buttermere, returning via the Whinlatter Pass (the climb towards Keswick is a long, slow drag) or Honister Pass (a short, sharp climb). See the Buttermere route for more details on Buttermere itself and the two passes.

Whatever you decide to do, the Newlands Valley is an excellent place to explore. There are fells to climb, good views and attractive villages. The valley is only a few miles long, but definitely worthy of your attention.

✦ From Keswick: from the central car park turn right onto the road, then left at the T-junction. Follow the road over the River Greta and take the lane off to the left a quarter of a mile after the houses finish. This leads to a narrow footbridge. Cross carefully on foot, then cycle up hill into Portinscale, passing the Derwent Water Hotel on the left. At the T-junction bear left.

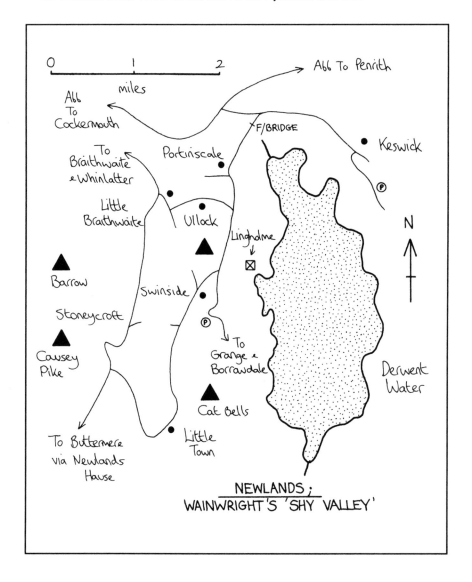

NEWLANDS;
WAINWRIGHT'S 'SHY VALLEY'

The road soon becomes surrounded by woodland. Half a mile after Portinscale look out for the driveway to Lingholm Gardens on the left. The gardens are open daily throughout summer, from 10am to 5pm. The house (not open) is a large Victorian mansion, where Beatrix Potter spent many holidays and made sketches of the grounds and views over Derwent Water, which she later incorporated in her tales. There is a tearoom and footpaths to the lake.

✦ Half a mile after Lingholm turn right, signposted 'Stair $^3/_4$ mile'.

The road rounds the Swinside plantation, giving good views of the fells to the left, most notably the plateau of Robinson which overlooks Buttermere. The road cuts through the village of Swinside, with Swinside Inn on the right, then passes through pleasant farmland in the bottom of the Newlands valley.

✦ Take the next left (before the hamlet of Stair) and follow the road to Little Town (1.25 miles).

On the immediate right is a row of small cottages, all named after local fells: Swinside, Robinson, Coledale etc, and on the left a telephone box. After black and white 'Ghyll Bank' the road bends tightly and dips over a small stream. Tree-lined Newlands Beck can be seen flowing from the head of the valley. Surprisingly it doesn't flow into Derwent Water, the nearest lake, but runs parallel to the River Derwent into Bassenthwaite Lake.

On the left now are the slopes and distinctive peak of Cat Bells, one of the most visited small fells of the area, which offers good views over the valley and over Derwent Water. There is a footpath to its summit from Little Town passing various mine workings. Newlands was once extensively mined (copper, lead and even gold) and many potentially dangerous shafts and levels still remain, so always stick to the obvious footpaths.

Little Town is a collection of fine white cottages nestling beneath the rocky outcrop of High Crags. The pyramidal fell on the other side of the valley is Causey Pike, 637 metres high, with excellent views in all directions. Footpaths to the summit from Stoneycroft, three-quarters of a mile north, are passed on the return journey to Keswick.

✦ After Little Town the road drops quite steeply. pass the small lay-by on the left and cross Newlands Beck via a small hump-backed bridge. The road follows the stream for a short way, then crosses over another arched bridge and begins to climb slightly to a T-junction with Rigg Beck (an unusual timbered house) on the right. There is a signpost: 'Buttermere 4 miles' to the left, 'Braithwaite $2^1/_4$ miles' to the right.

✦ [For Buttermere: turn left and follow the road along the slopes of the Derwent Fells, climbing gradually towards Newlands Hause. There is a steep stretch after Keskadale Farm, then a steady climb through an empty valley, running alongside Keskadale Beck. The only severe climb is the final quarter mile up to the pass, after which there is over a mile of steep descent into Buttermere.]

✦ To complete the short Newlands circuit and head back to Keswick, turn right at 'Rigg Beck'.

The Newlands Valley

The road crosses a stream on a tight bend and then runs along the fellside, unfenced and open on the left. At Stoneycroft (National Trust owned) there is an unusual stone bridge crossing Stoneycroft Gill, a fine mountain stream with plenty of large rocks to sit on to paddle or picnic. Slightly further up-hill there is a bench looking over the valley to the conifer plantation on Swinside. The footpath alongside the stream, once used by the miners that worked on the fells, leads up to Causey Pike.

✦ Follow the open road, cross over the cattle grid and take the first sharp right (just over 1 mile from Stoneycroft) signed 'Swinside 1 mile'.

The road drops down quite steeply through the farm buildings of Little Braithwaite.

✦ Take the first left turning signed 'Ullock', follow the road, which circles Swinside (fell) and becomes enclosed by trees. At the junction bear left, signed 'Portinscale 3/4 mile'.

✦ [Alternatively, to increase the route to include a circuit of Derwent Water, turn right and keep straight ahead until the lake comes into view in about 1 mile.] (For more information see the Derwent Water route.)

For Keswick, turn right in Portinscale and return via the same route: downhill to the footbridge, turning right onto the road for the town centre.

KESWICK TO CALDBECK

"BACK A' SKIDDA'"

Starting point: Central car park, Keswick (NY265234).

Distance: 35 miles.

Terrain: Some stretches on busy roads, some very quiet narrow lanes, some fairly steep sections. No off-road cycling.

Maps: OS Landranger 90, Touring Map 3.

Public Toilets: Dodd Wood car park, on A591, and that's about it. You'll have to rely on pubs.

Refreshments: Keswick: pubs, cafés, restaurants; Old Saw Mill Tearoom, Dodd Wood; various village inns.

There is a good deal of effort needed for this route, and a few miles are (unavoidably) along the busy A591. It is included for those who like to get away from it all, as the Uldale and Caldbeck Fells behind Skiddaw are very quiet, if not lonely fells; practically unknown to the tourist. The route passes through several Cumbrian villages, each with its own inn, a few cottages and not much else: very rural villages, what Wainwright would describe as 'charming'. There is little by way of tourist attractions along the way, but this is the route for anyone wishing to escape from it all on a busy bank holiday.

For a full day out this route can easily be adapted to include the Whinlatter/Lorton/Wythop route, thus avoiding the A591 altogether.

✦ From the central car park in Keswick turn right onto the road and bear left at the T-junction. Follow the road and turn right after the river and Pencil Museum. Continue to the roundabout (half a mile) and take the second exit along the A591.

After 3 miles you will come to Mirehouse on the left, home of the Spedding family when they moved here from Armathwaite Hall further around the lake. The house was built in 1666 and was visited by many famous people including Wordsworth, fellow Lake Poet Southey and the poet Tennyson. There is often live piano music to be heard which adds to the romantic effect of the house. The grounds are open daily through-out the season (Easter to October). The house itself is restricted to Wednesdays, Sundays and Bank Holiday Mondays, 2pm to 5pm.

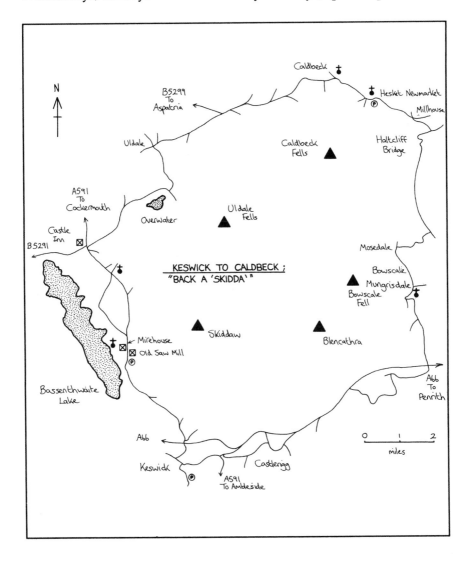

A short way from Mirehouse, along a public footpath close to the gates, is the Church of Saint Bega, which stands overlooking the lake. Originally built in the 10th century, probably on a former ancient site, which explains its unusual circular graveyard. The footpath continues to a lane which runs to the right back up to the A591, but the easiest option is to retrace your steps to Mirehouse. Directly over the road is the Dodd Wood car park where there are toilets and forest walks, leading eventually up to Skiddaw if you've got the time and energy. To the left of the car park is the Old Sawmill Tearoom, open daily 10.30 to 5.30.

Bassenthwaite Lake from Dodd Wood

✦ Either continue along the main road, or turn left after Mirehouse along a narrow lane, after 1 mile turn right for another mile, then bear left onto the main road for yet another mile. Take the right turning directly before the Castle Inn, signposted 'Uldale 3 miles'. Take the first right turning (2 miles) signed for Overwater Hall hotel.

From the Castle Inn the road rises quite steeply for about 1.5 miles, after which it undulates fairly regularly. There is a downhill drop towards Overwater, on the right, quite a pleasant tarn with trees around its southern fringes and the unmistakable outline of Skiddaw visible in the distance. This little-known tarn is not actually accessible to the public. It is less than half a mile long and is dammed at the northern end as it is now used as a reservoir. Beyond it are the Uldale Fells, which Wainwright recommends for busy days, as even on a Bank Holiday you can walk for miles and meet no one.

✦ After Overwater turn left signed to Uldale.

Uphill again. The countryside here is quite bare, much less dramatic than the more popular areas within the Natural Park,

✦ Cross over the River Ellen and pass through the hamlet of Stanthwaite (beware of mud on road). Follow the road as it climbs the last half mile to Uldale. Turn right at the cross roads, signed 'Caldbeck $5^1/_4$ miles'.

Uldale is a farming community which grew up in the 18th century. It is surrounded by wide walled fields, is very rural and sees few tourists. The village pub 'The Snooty Fox' is on the left. After the village the road begins to climb steadily. After a cattle grid it crosses open moorland, not the sort of scenery normally associated with Lakeland. These are the empty Uldale Fells. The road is straight and visible for miles, moving gradually in steps downhill.

✦ Carry on straight ahead following the signs for Caldbeck.

After Parkend (restaurant) on the right the road is contained between hawthorn hedges and there are considerably more trees.

✦ Continue into Caldbeck.

The Oddfellows Arms (formerly 'The John Peel') is on the left, though you may have to take a backwards glance to see it: a black and white building with colourful window boxes. Then pass the church of Saint Kentigern built on the site of Saint Mungo's Well. Mungo was an affectionate nickname for Saint Kentigern, and turns up in several place names, such as Mungrisdale. In the churchyard is the grave of 'Mary of Buttermere', a young woman who married a con-man. The tale was novelized and became a bestseller. The author was none other than Melvyn Bragg, who lives at High Ireby, not far from here.

Shortly after the church, on the left, is the 'Priest's Mill' with a café and craft shop.

Caldbeck is famous for being the home of the legendary huntsman John Peel, who was born here in 1776, by all accounts an arrogant and unpleasant man, and not at all a local hero. It also has the distinction of being the most northerly village in the Lake District. The Caldbeck Fells to the south have been mined since the 16th century, for a variety of metals and minerals (23 in all) including copper, lead and zinc. The village has its own mining museum, which must make it one of the most touristy venues of the whole Northern fells area. From the museum, guided tours around local mines can be arranged. The fells are littered with disused shafts and levels which are dangerous and should never be entered without expert assistance.

✦ Continue past the cricket club on the left, along a flat road into Hesket Newmarket.

As its name suggests, Hesket Newmarket was once an important market. It now remains a pleasant village of attractive cottages grouped around a central green. The village inn, the Old Crown, is on the right in the middle of a terraced row.

✦ Follow the road through the village, signed 'Millhouse 1¹/₄ miles'.

This is a more fertile area of pastures with plenty of trees. The road for the most part follows the course of the River Caldew, which flows down from Skiddaw heading for Carlisle.

✦ In Millhouse turn right, signed 'Haltcliff Bridge 1¹/₄ miles'. The road winds between houses and becomes tree-lined. At the T-junction bear right, signed 'Haltcliff Bridge ¹/₂ mile'.

There is a steep downhill stretch (1:7) after Haltcliff and a sharp turn to the left. The road becomes very narrow and there are high grassy banks and hedges on both sides, though there are still views in some places towards Skiddaw.

✦ Take the second right turning (2 miles after Haltcliff Bridge) along a narrow winding lane, passing Low Mill and crossing over the River Caldew. Follow the lane (passing through 3 gates) into Mosedale.

Mosedale is a small, isolated hamlet at the end of the valley of the same name. Among its buildings is a Quaker Meeting House, built in 1702, where refreshments are sometimes served.

✦ Bear left in Mosedale and follow the road into Mungrisdale (1.25 miles).

The road again crosses the River Caldew, formed from tributaries that flow down from the Skiddaw range. On the left of the road is the flat valley bottom (riverless at this point) and on the right is Bowscale Fell (702 metres). From the hamlet of Bowscale there is a footpath and bridleway up to Bowscale Tarn, Wainwright's favourite Lakeland tarn.

Mungrisdale takes its name from Saint Mungo, his name being tacked onto the common Lakeland name of Grisedale, meaning the dale of wild pigs. The quaint Mill Inn was built in the 16th century and was visited by Charles Dickens on his tour of the Lakes. The small church was built in the mid-18th century to replace a much older building, and as at Caldbeck it is dedicated to Saint Mungo.

✦ Continue through the village. ilgnore the right turning for the Mill Inn and follow the road as it bends tightly and crosses the River Glenderamackin. Continue past Beckside to the main road (just under 2 miles).

✦ EITHER bear right along the A66, which drops down steadily into Keswick.

✦ OR, to avoid the main road, there are various short detours which can be taken: cross the main road and take the lane opposite. Take the second left (after 1.5 miles). After another 1.5 miles this loops around and rejoins the busy A66. Bear left towards Keswick. Again either remain on the A66 and follow the signs for Keswick, or take the second turning on the left, for a longer, more strenuous, but peaceful detour via Castlerigg stone circle. Pass Burns Farm and take the second left over Naddle Bridge. Bear left again, heading quite steeply uphill for half a mile. Pass Goosewell Farm on the right, after which is a lay-by for Castlerigg.

The stone circle is in the middle of a walled field on the left of the lane. There are 38 stones of varying size and shape which form the circle itself. It was built in the Bronze Age, about 3,500 years ago, long before the Druids, who are usually credited with the construction of such monuments. There is still no concrete evidence to prove what the purpose of stone circles was: gathering places, religious temples, stone age 'observatories' or energy centres? Castlerigg is on a plain surrounded by high fells, including Blencathra and Skiddaw. It is now in the care of the National Trust.

✦ From Castlerigg follow the lane downhill and turn left onto the main road. At the junction bear right and follow the road into Keswick town centre. Take the left turning directly after the telephone boxes and follow the road round to the car park.

Castlerigg Stone Circle

THIRLMERE

THE DROWNED VALLEY

Starting point: Steel End car park, Wythburn (NY321129) at southern end of reservoir.

Distance: 12 miles

Terrain: Roads, mainly flat; quite a busy main road along one side of the lake which is unavoidable.

Maps: OS Outdoor Leisure 4 or 5; OS Landranger 90; OS Lake District Touring Map

Public Toilets: Dob Gill Car Park, on western shore; Armboth car park, on western shore; the Swirls car park, near Thirlspot on eastern shore

---

✦ **To reach Thirlmere from Ambleside:** follow the A591 past Grasmere and up the slow climb to Dunmail Raise (the body of King Dunmail supposedly lies where he fell in battle, beneath a cairn of stones, now on the central reserve). The road then begins to drop steadily with glimpses of the reservoir ahead. There is a short stretch of dual carriageway. Turn left 1 mile after this. The Steel End car park is in the trees on the right.

✦ **To reach Thirlmere from Keswick:** Again, follow the A591 from the town centre, bear right after the stretch of dual carriageway for the northern end of the reservoir, or continue along the A591, following the route description in reverse.

This simple route around the reservoir of Thirlmere is included for completeness, and because Thirlmere today is actually quite picturesque, except for the busy A591 that runs along one side, the main route between Ambleside and Keswick.

The route follows the only available roads around the water and can be started from any of the various car parks along the reservoir. To avoid traffic on the main road, do that leg of the journey first, ideally early on a Sunday morning, then follow the road along the western shore at a leisurely pace.

✦ From the car park at Steel End turn left onto the road.

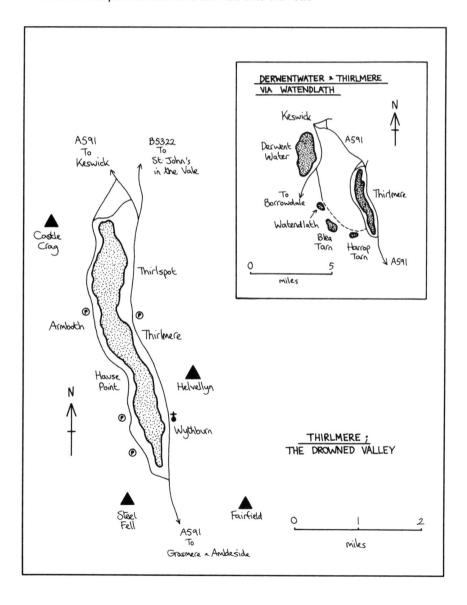

DERWENTWATER & THIRLMERE
VIA WATENDLATH

Keswick

Derwent Water

A591

To Borrowdale

Watendlath

Blea Tarn

Thirlmere

Harrop Tarn

A591

N

0   5
miles

A591
To
Keswick

B5322
To
St John's
in the Vale

Castle Crag

Thirlspot

Armboth

Thirlmere

Hause Point

Helvellyn

N

Wythburn

THIRLMERE ;
THE DROWNED VALLEY

Steel Fell

A591
To
Grasmere & Ambleside

Fairfield

0   1   2
miles

There are over 50 streams running into Thirlmere. The footpath from this car park leads to two of the major tributaries, Raise Beck and Wyth Burn, which enter the reservoir at its head. The second of these becks gave its name to a village that stood close by, which is now lost beneath the water. The valley's original lake was hour-glass shaped, with a series of wooden bridges crossing its narrowest point. This lake was sometimes classed as two individual lakes and given the names Leathes Water and Wythburn Water, but in 1803 Coleridge wrote of "O Thirlmere" and in 1877 John Ruskin wrote to 'The Times' accusing the Manchester Corporation of "plotting to steal the waters of Thirlmere", so the name, which means 'the lake with the hollow', has obviously been in occasional use for some time, and was not, as many try to suggest, an invention of Manchester Corporation when they dammed the valley.

◆ Bear left at the junction onto the A591. This is a busy road, so exercise caution. Continue half a mile to Wythburn church on the right.

The church is all that remains of the village of Wythburn (pronounced 'Wyburn'). It is essentially a 17th century building with Victorian additions. It stands on higher ground than the homes of its parishioners and thus escaped the water when it came. In the trees directly over the road are the ruins of The Nags Head Inn, where Keats once stayed while touring the Lakes.

◆ From the church continue north along the A591.

By the telephone box just after the church is one of the many memorial stones erected by Canon Rawnsley, this one being in memory of the poet, Matthew Arnold, who stayed at the 'Nags Head' and wrote of his journeys through "the cheerful silence of the fells" to the west of Thirlmere in his poem 'Resignation'.

Half a mile after The Nags Head stood its opposition, The Cherry Tree Inn where Wordsworth once stopped to give an impromptu recital of some of his works.

Three-quarters of a mile after the church you may notice in the trees on the left what appears to be the turret of a castle. This is the Straining Well Pumping Station, designed so as not to intrude on the landscape. If only all such structures were so inoffensive. You have to give it to the water people, at least they tried.

It was just after the pumping station that the 'Rock of Names' once stood. This was an outcrop of rock where Wordsworth and Coleridge often met, being roughly the half-way point between their homes in Grasmere and Keswick. The poets and their entourage carved their names in the face of the stone, which remained there from the turn of the 19th century until 1886, when the rock had to be blown up to make way for the new road when the reservoir was under construction. Canon Rawnsley tried desperately to save it from destruction and when he failed, he tried to have the initials chiselled intact from the rock face. This also proved impossible. The rock was duly blown up and another piece of history was lost . . . at least it would have been, had the good Canon not collected all the relevant pieces together and made them into a small cairn to mark the spot where the original rock once stood. They remained there for almost a century, until 1984, when they were moved to Dove Cottage and reassembled, protected for posterity.

A short way ahead, there are parking areas on either side of the road. On the left there are views over Thirlmere and a path down through the trees to the water's edge. In the car park on the other side there are public toilets and paths up to Helvellyn, said to be the most-climbed high fell in the Lake District. Wainwright felt there was a "mystical quality" about Helvellyn, and that its "lovely name is a magnet". Its popularity is probably more due to it being one of the most conveniently-placed mountains for the motorist, with a car park at its base.

Also from this car park is the newly created Swirls Forest Trail, extending in a southerly direction at the base of Helvellyn. There should be a leaflet available in the car park.

✦ From the car park return to the main road and continue north. Pass the King's Head at Thirlspot and continue for another mile, then bear left.

Manchester Corporation sent men out on horseback to find a suitable site for the new reservoir that they desperately needed. They chose Thirlmere and a raging debate began. The Thirlmere Defence Society was born overnight, backed by many famous names, including John Ruskin and the ever-present Canon Rawnsley. Regardless of the great opposition to the scheme, Parliament (no surprises here) sided with Manchester Corporation and the valley was flooded. As a direct result of this failure to save the old Thirlmere, Canon Rawnsley set about forming a national society which would preserve the landscape and care for buildings of historic interest. This society still exists today. We know it as the National Trust.

✦ Pass the campsite on the left and follow the road across the Thirlmere dam.

Thirlmere today is 3.5 miles long. It was created when a dam was built across the northern end of the Wythburn valley, preventing the outflow of the many mountain streams that come down from the heights of Helvellyn on the eastern shore and Armboth Fell on the west. This road crosses the dam at the foot of the reservoir, the first stone of which was laid on 2nd August 1890. Looking over the edge into the water is quite eerie – the water looks black and bottomless. It is 158 feet at its deepest, the water level of the original lake(s) having risen by 54 feet. On the right as you're crossing the dam is another of those castellated towers: the Water Board disguising their buildings. You have to admit, it's better than the squat, pre-fabricated bunkers they use elsewhere.

Helvellyn (and mist) seen across Thirlmere

✦ After the dam, follow the road around to the left along the western shore.

The water from Thirlmere travels 96 miles to Manchester in an underground conduit, flowing downhill all the way, so as to avoid the cost of having it pumped. It collects in a holding reservoir at Heaton Park, North Manchester, and from there it is piped into peoples' homes.

1.5 miles after the dam is Armboth car park, where there are toilets and access to the lake. Somewhere out under the water close to here are the remains of Armboth House, reputed to be haunted by a murdered bride who endlessly prepares for the wedding feast that never occurred. A stranded monkey puzzle tree on the shore, now sadly out of place amongst the conifers, once stood in the garden.

✦ Continue along the road, heading south.

The fells around Thirlmere today are almost entirely covered with dense plantations. The trees are not native to this country, and at the time of planting many people objected to them. It was believed they would encourage rainfall and keep the water-level topped up. This proved not to be the case, though they do trap mist, and long after the mist has cleared from elsewhere there are white trails of it hanging over the surface of Thirlmere . . . or could it be wind-borne remnants of the wedding dress of that poor murdered bride who was consigned to a watery grave . . .

The trees on the right of the road hide the stone ruins of structures that existed on the edge of the drowned community: walled fields, cart tracks, barns and outbuildings, all overgrown and lost within the forest.

2 miles after Armboth, there are toilets at the Dob Gill car park on the right. This is also the start of various forest trails. Again there should be leaflets in a wooden box by the toilet block. One path (actually a bridleway) leads up through the trees alongside the gill and its waterfall (according to Coleridge the *loudest* waterfall in Lakeland) to Harrop Tarn, a small, reedy lake. From here mountain bikers and hardy cyclists can follow the track to the right, passing Blea Tarn on the left, joining a lane at Watendlath. This road leads down towards Derwent Water crossing the popular Ashness Bridge. If cameras caused erosion the bridge would no longer be with us. It appears on EVERY Lakeland calendar, along with Tarn Hows, near Hawkshead. Bear right towards Keswick, and in the town centre follow the A591 (for Ambleside) back to Thirlmere.

✦ Continue along the road for the final mile back to the Steel End car park on the left.

The Eastern Lakes

ULLSWATER

THE WESTERN SHORE

Starting point: Glenridding car park (NY386161)

Distance: 20 miles/12 miles via ferry

Terrain: Roads, some steep sections, a large proportion on busy A-roads.

Maps: OS Landranger 90; OS Lakes Touring Map; OS Outdoor Leisure Map 5

Public Toilets: Glenridding: main car park, at junction of A592 and A5091.

Refreshments: Glenridding: café on main road; Dacre: pub.

✦ From Penrith to Ullswater: follow signs from the town centre for A66 bound for Keswick. After 1 mile take the A592 which runs along the western shore of the lake.

✦ From Windermere to Ullswater: from the railway station turn right and join the main road, turn left and drop downhill to a roundabout. Take the last exit along the A592 for Ullswater and follow the road all the way to the lake. This is an excellent (if tiring) ride via the Kirkstone Pass and Brothers Water. For a more detailed description of this route see 'Town Links' section at the end of the book.

There are few roads around the Ullswater area, which means that the use of busy A-roads is, unfortunately, unavoidable. The A592 runs the entire length of the lake on the western shore, and is the only road anywhere near to the water. However, it is a pleasant road with some excellent views over Ullswater and the surrounding fells, and between Glenridding and Waterfoot it is relatively flat. I only said 'relatively' – it isn't flat, but there are no great climbs. At the right time of day the traffic can (almost) be avoided.

The narrow lanes between Matterdale End and Dacre are very pleasant, through a quiet and unspoilt landscape (the tourists seem to stick to the lakeside and the high fells) but it demands more exertion. This route can be tailored to suit your needs. If you want to avoid either the steep hills or nearly 8 miles of A-road then the Ullswater ferry is for you, operating a full service in the season (more or less hourly) and a reduced service out of season. To check on the timetable telephone 07684-82229. They can be boarded from piers at Glenridding and close to Pooley Bridge.

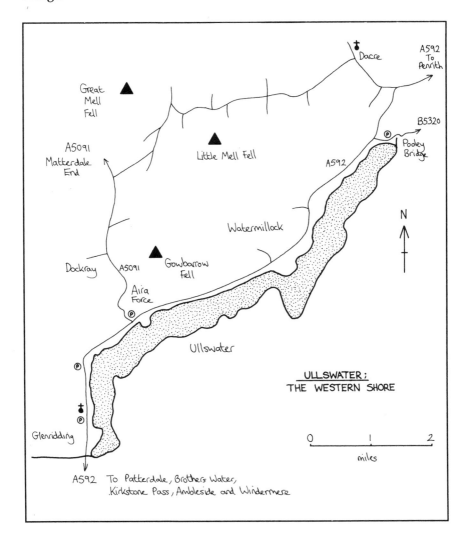

✦ From Glenridding's main car park, turn left onto the main road (A592).

The road winds continually, with a sheer rock face on the left and a small woodland of beech trees close to the water's edge on the right. It's well worth stopping here for a 5 minute walk through the trees to the lakeside.

✦ After 2 miles turn left along the A5091, signed for 'Dockray $1^1/_4$'.

There are public toilets on the opposite corner here. The road climbs steadily, away from the lake. On the right is a small car park for Aira Force, probably the best known and most visited Lakeland waterfall. There is a short walk through trees to the Force itself, now managed by the National Trust. The water drops 70 feet down a wooded ravine, an impressive sight, especially after heavy rain. Wordsworth and Coleridge visited the Force while on a walking tour together in 1799. Coleridge moaned because there was too much water and there was nowhere suitable to view it from! Today, the National Trust have made it into what must be the district's most accessible waterfall, in that you can walk all around it and see it from all angles, even though it is somewhat 'pedestrianized' and gets very busy at weekends.

✦ Continue along the main road to Dockray ($^3/_4$ mile).

The approach to Dockray is downhill between trees. A bridge crosses over Aira Beck at the centre of the small village. On the left is the Royal Hotel. On the right are views over the Aira Beck valley to Gowbarrow Fell, a short climb and a good vantage point for Ullswater, best reached from a path close to Aira Force.

✦ Continue through Dockray to Matterdale End (1.25 miles). Pass the telephone box in the centre of the village and then turn right, signed to Penruddock.

The road curves uphill slightly around Great Mell Fell, a rounded hill partially covered with trees. The forest to the left contains a military rifle range, so gun shots should be expected.

✦ Avoid the first right turning back to Dockray. Take the second right, signed for 'Thackthwaite 1 mile'. Follow the road as it crosses over a stream and climbs quite steeply for a short way. Keep left.

On the right are the slopes of Little Mell Fell, which Wainwright condemns harshly as being "an uninspiring, unattractive, bare and rounded hump". If you should still want to aim for the summit after such a scathing review, the best way from this side is along a path running close to the stream near Thackthwaite. The fell is only 31 metres smaller than its counterpart, Great Mell Fell.

✦ Avoid the left turning to Thackthwaite and follow the road over a stream, climbing quite steeply uphill.

The road continues as a tree-lined lane, giving views to the left over bare flat fields, and ahead are the high hills of the Pennines.

✦ After the drive to Grovefoot Farm the road drops down gradually to a cross-roads. Head straight across, signed 'Dacre 1^1/$_2$ miles'. The road continues mainly downhill. After 'High Bridge' the road bears right and leads into Dacre village.

Dacre is a pleasant enough village of old stone and concrete, though not generally frequented by the tourist. The castle, visible from the road, was built in the 14th century as a defence against the Scots, and restored in the 16th. It is not open to the public, but can be seen easily enough from the road. The church, behind the village to the left, is essentially of Norman construction, believed to occupy the site of a pre-Viking monastery. Four Anglo-Saxon stone bears, supposedly from the castle roof, can be seen in the churchyard, one standing in each corner. Close to the church there is a footpath leading behind the castle across the fields to 'Dalemain' (1 mile) a Georgian-fronted Elizabethan mansion with views down to Ullswater. It is open to the public 11.15am to 5pm, Sunday to Thursday, April to October. Apart from the house itself there are gardens and parkland, museums, gift shop and restaurant. The Lake District doesn't have that many stately homes, and this is considered by many to be the best.

✦ Turn right in Dacre, signed for 'Ullswater 2 miles'.

There are views to the right of Little Mell Fell. The road narrows and bears right over a stream, then climbs steeply (1:8). Views again to the left over to the Pennines, then the road begins to drop downhill.

✦ At the main road bear right for Glenridding.

✦ For the ferry back to Glenridding follow the main road for 1 mile and bear left towards Pooley Bridge. Follow the water-side road a quarter of a mile to the pier.

The main road enters an area of woodland close to the shore of the lake. There are various large country house hotels on the water's edge in this area, but none to rival the opulence and indulgence of the world famous Sharrow Bay Hotel on the opposite shore, opened in 1948 by two bachelors, an example to country house hotels everywhere. The rooms are bursting with genuine antiques and are given women's names rather than numbers. But don't try rolling up with your bike and your rucksack – this is a sophisticated hotel!

The main road winds often, undulating frequently, but not severely, passing through the scattered community of Watermillock, shortly after which the road returns to the water's edge and runs close to it for most of the way back to Glenridding, with some excellent views of the opposite shore.

✦ Pass the junction with the A5091 (toilets on the corner) and continue into Glenridding.

Ullswater and one of its ferries

ULLSWATER

GLENRIDDING TO HOWTOWN: A LAKESIDE RIDE

Starting point: Glenridding car park (NY386161)

Distance: 22 miles maximum (depending on route taken)

Terrain: Roads, some busy(can be avoided by ferry); quiet lanes with one steep climb and steep bridleways for mountain bikers (optional).

Maps: OS Landranger 90; OS Lakes Touring Map; OS Outdoor Leisure Map 5.

Public Toilets: Glenridding car park; junction of A592 and A5091; Pooley Bridge.

Refreshments: Glenridding: café, pubs; Pooley Bridge: cafés, pubs, restaurants

✦ **From Penrith to Glenridding:** follow the A66 bound for Keswick, after about 1 mile switching to the A592 which runs alongside Ullswater. The road leads directly into the village. The main car park is on the right.

✦ **From Windermere/Glenridding to Glenridding:** follow the A592 to Ullswater, via the Kirkstone Pass (see 'Town Links' at the end of the book for a more detailed route description). The road leads directly into Glenridding village. The central car park is on the left.

As with the last route, this one demands several miles along a busy A-road, unless you take the ferry the entire length of the lake and cycle back on the quieter eastern shore. This road does not continue the entire length of the lake, so after spending some time exploring the area, particularly the excellent viewpoint of Hallin Fell, either catch the ferry back to Glenridding from the pier at Howtown, or continue along Boredale or Bannerdale, following the bridle-paths back to Glenridding. Again, this route is quite adaptable and can be tailored to suit your needs, your time and your energy. Cycles are free on the ferries providing there is enough room. To check times and availability phone: 0539-721626. This route would begin suitably well from Pooley Bridge or even Martindale on the eastern shore.

✦ Start in Glenridding's main car park. Turn left onto the A592.

Glenridding, apart from its setting, is rather unspectacular. It grew up as a lead mining village, but the mines closed in the 'sixties and it has now been taken over by Lakeland's favourite industry: Tourism. That said, there are still relatively few amenities here: a café, a very practical general store and a couple of hotels. The car park also houses the new toilet block and Tourist Information Centre.

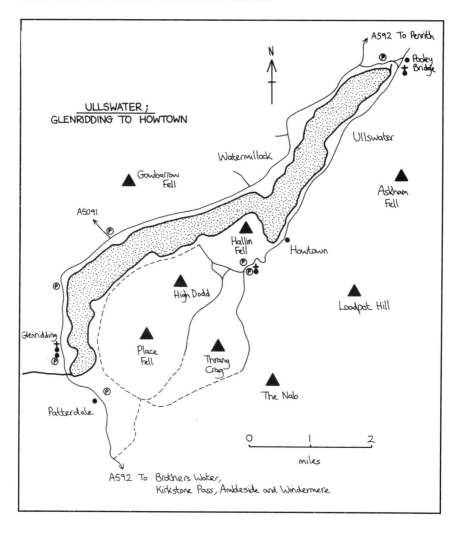

Perhaps Glenridding's claim to fame is as the southern terminal for the Ullswater ferries. If you have chosen to avoid the A-road and travel to Pooley Bridge on the water, bear right out of the car park and take the first left, clearly signed for the pier. The two steamers, *Raven* and *Lady of the Lake* were launched over a century ago and plough up and down the lake regularly throughout the season.

Just after the village on the right there are some attractive beech woodlands along the shore with footpaths along the water, which certainly merit at least a short visit. There are several strategically placed benches which offer excellent views over the lake.

Ullswater is the second largest of the sixteen lakes, being 7.5 miles long with a bend in the middle. It was actually on the shores of Ullswater that William and Dorothy Wordsworth encountered the famous daffodils immortalized by the poet, and not in Grasmere or Rydal as is popularly believed. Wordsworth and Wainwright agree that Ullswater is probably the most beautiful of all the lakes in Lakeland.

✦ Continue along the A592, which undulates fairly regularly (but not too steeply) and winds continually at first. Take care on the tight bends.

There are public toilets at the junction with the A5091, after which there are various paths leading uphill for half a mile to Aira Force, probably Lakeland's most famous, most visited waterfall, now in the care of the National Trust. In a wooded glen the water drops 70 feet down a cleft in the rock. It is also one of the Lake District's most accessible waterfalls, as you can walk right round it on one of the various paths and view it from several angles.

Shortly after the toilets on the left, the road crosses Aira Beck on its way down from the falls to the lake, after which is 'Lyulph's Tower', a Gothic sham: a Georgian manor built in 1780 to serve as a hunting lodge, with false fortifications to give it the appearance of being a small castle.

✦ Continue along the A592 through the scattered community of Watermillock. For the final half mile of the lake the road runs alongside the water. Take the next right along the B5320 for Pooley Bridge.

The road follows the foot of the lake. A quarter of a mile along is the northern steamer pier. Further along there are car parks on both sides of the road. The first settlement here, believed to be Celtic, was on the small wooded fell to the west of the river, the remains of which can still be seen among the trees. Today the popular tourist village of Pooley Bridge lies on the eastern bank of the River Eamont, the outflow of Ullswater. It is a pleasant village, mainly 18th century, busy throughout the season and has all the usual tourist features: a couple of tearooms, gift shops, B&B's and pubs. It was here, in his mid-twenties that Wainwright spent his first night ever in a hotel.

✦ Turn right directly after the church and then right again at the small crossroads.

This quiet road runs close to the shore for almost half the length of Ullswater. It is narrow in parts, undulating constantly, though not severely and winding its way between the trees. After 2 miles you may see a sign for Sharrow Bay one of Lakeland's (and in fact England's) most prestigious hotels, overlooking the lake, where the famous and filthy rich can indulge themselves. Another 1.5 miles brings you to the hamlet of Howtown, where you will find Ullswater's third ferry stage. From here you can travel to Glenridding or Pooley Bridge. There is also a good path around the base of Hallin Fell.

Towards Bannerdale from Hallin Fell, eastern shore

✦ Either return to Glenridding via the ferry or, to continue, follow the road through Howtown which rises steadily and soon leads to a serious climb where the road zig-zags tightly. This hard ascent leads to Martindale.

At the top of the pass there are parking spaces and Saint Peter's church, built in 1882 to replace a much older, much smaller church at the head of Bannerdale.

Opposite Saint Peter's is the well-trodden path up to Hallin Fell, a short climb that should not be missed, as it is an excellent viewpoint over almost the entire length of Ullswater. From the summit cairn (which is actually a short tower structure) there is a clear view along the lake to Penrith in the north-east, and to the south the valleys of Bannerdale and Boredale . These two valleys run almost parallel, with Beda Fell between. The valley bottoms are fertile pastures which end abruptly at the beginning of the slopes. At the entrance to Bannerdale, on the left, stands the old church of Saint Martin's, built in 1633, at one time left for dead, now renewed, restored and in full working order.

✦ Boredale/Bannerdale to Boredale Hause: which ever valley you choose, the route is simple to follow. Recommended for mountain bikers only, though it is not impossible to haul a racer up the fells. Continue along the road until it ends, then follow the bridleway uphill. Boredale Hause is a meeting point of many paths and bridleways. Carefully follow the bridleway leading downhill to the left, heading away from the lake. In three-quarters of a mile you should come to a T-junction with another bridleway. Bear right, then left almost immediately, crossing the stream and joining the A592 at Deepdale Bridge. Bear right along the road.

✦ Alternatively, to return to Howtown from Boredale Hause, follow the bridleway to the right around the lower slopes of Place Fell. When this eventually joins the road bear right and then left, following the road back through Martindale to Howtown, and catch the ferry over to Glenridding.

POOLEY BRIDGE TO HAWESWATER

THE FAR EAST

Starting point: Pooley Bridge (NY472245). There are two car parks just before the village, one on either side of the river. Either will suffice.

Distance: 25 – 28 miles, depending on route taken.

Terrain: Quiet roads, gently undulating for the most part, some brief climbs. Optional off-road route across Moor Divock.

Maps: OS Landranger 90; OS Outdoor Leisure 5; OS Touring Map 3

Refreshments: Pooley Bridge: tearooms, pubs; various village pubs along the way.

✦ **To Pooley Bridge from Penrith:** follow signs for the A66, heading west for Keswick, then join the A592 for Ullswater. After 4 miles bear left for Pooley Bridge.

✦ **To Pooley Bridge from Windermere:** from the railway station turn right and join the A591, dropping down towards the lake. After 1 mile is a roundabout. Take the last exit along the A592. This road climbs steadily to the Kirkstone Pass and then drops down to Ullswater. Bear right after the lake for Pooley Bridge.

This route makes use of miles of quiet lanes between the far eastern fells of the Lake District, which for some reason, like the northern fells, are not generally frequented by the tourist. Unlike the northern fells, however, the countryside in the east is usually green and fertile, especially the lush Lowther Valley. It is certainly an area worth visiting.

✦ Start in Pooley Bridge. There are two routes to choose from. Firstly, for mountain bikers or hardy cyclists the bridleway up to Moor Divock. Take the right turning directly after the church. Continue straight across at the cross roads: a narrow lane leading uphill between a few scattered farmsteads. The road deteriorates into a trackway, climbing steadily. Pass 'Roehead' on the left and continue along the open track across the fellside to the flat plateau of Moor Divock (³/₄ mile).

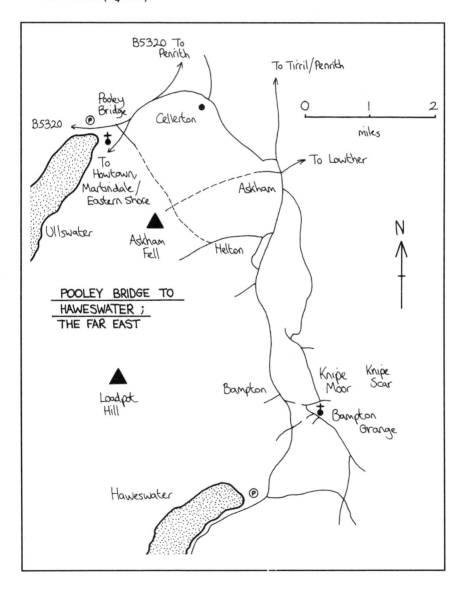

The lush Lowther Valley

Anyone interested in pre-history should not miss Moor Divock: several miles of open grassy moorland which is littered with burial mounds and standing stones, and a wide circle (30 feet diameter) of low stones, called The Cock-Pit. Also, from later in history, the Roman road 'High Street' cuts across the moor on its way to the fort at Brougham, outside Penrith.

✦ Continue along the bridleway, cutting straight across the moor, crossing an open road and heading downhill. Shortly after the road the trackway becomes a narrow lane leading down to a junction. Bear right and follow the valley road.

✦ Alternatively, to avoid the bridleway, from Pooley Bridge follow the main road through the village, heading away from Ullswater. After 1 mile bear right, signed for Celleron. The road rises steadily. Keep right.

This is limestone country. the fields on either side of the road are edged with white dry-stone walls. On the right is Heughscar Hill on which the limestone is exposed in places.

◆ At the T-junction bear right and drop down into Askham and follow the road through the village.

You may notice over to the left on the approach to the village a castle-like building backed by trees. This is Askham Hall. Like so many Lakeland mansions it was developed from a defensive pele tower, parts of it date back to the 1300s. It is now the home of the Duke of Lonsdale.

Askham, with many 17th century cottages, is considered to be amongst the prettiest villages in Cumbria. The houses are set beyond wide grass verges which keep them well away from the road, though there are also modern and unattractive additions to the edges of the village. The Queen's Head inn is on the right. Make a brief detour to the left to visit Saint Peter's church or Lowther Castle, built in 1802 as a Gothic mansion, which proved too expensive to maintain. The interior was demolished as it became unsafe, and today only an impressive facade remains.

◆ A quarter of a mile after Askham is a fork in the road. Keep right, signed for Bampton.

On the left is the fertile basin of a river valley and there are fine views over its woodlands and fields. The next village encountered is Helton. The road passes the Helton Inn and a turning to the right leads up to the village centre. Continuing through the valley the road becomes narrower, passing Beckfoot Country House Hotel on the right, then crosses over a bridge at Butterwick. The road continues, relatively flat, between hedges and comes into Bampton, an attractive village of black and white houses, where you will find Saint Patrick's Well Inn.

◆ Just after the village, bear right, signed 'Haweswater and Mardale'. The road is at first quite flat and in half a mile climbs to a crossroads. Continue straight ahead for the reservoir.

The road continues climbing, between stone walls and trees, with good views to the left. After passing Thornthwaite Hall on the left, the road drops gently into an area of attractive woodland.

◆ Keep left, following signs for Haweswater.

You may get glimpses of the reservoir through the trees on the right, and should be able to see the large dam, built in the mid-fifties to collect water for Manchester. (Thirlmere suffered the same fate). There is a plaque on the right, commemorating the day, 5th October 1957, when water from two local streams was diverted into the waiting reservoir. The original Haweswater was a small lake that was dammed and swelled beyond all recognition, taking beneath its waters the village of Mardale Green and filling the entire basin of the valley. Wainwright was familiar with the original Haweswater and Mardale Green. The last time he saw the village, its pub, The Dun Bull and cottages were derelict and awaiting demolition.

Haweswater reservoir (quite low)

Around the edge of the reservoir is a white rim of small stones, apparently caused by the continual rise and fall of the water, uncovering the bedrock. Many say this white border makes Haweswater look so obviously man-made – sterile and artificial, but the valley of Mardale is surprisingly picturesque and is surrounded by some of the finest fells in the whole of the Lake District.

◆ There is only one road to Mardale Head at the southern end of the reservoir, so the return journey must be made the same way. The road keeps close to the water's edge, passing the Haweswater Hotel on the left and eventually dropping down to the car park at the head of Haweswater.

Much of this road is tree-lined, though there are views through the trees and over the water. Three-quarters of the way along the lake is a water-tower, built in a Gothic style, striding out into the water.

At Mardale Head, there is nothing now but a car park. The lost village of Mardale Green stood close-by, and in exceptionally dry weather the stone walls and foundations belonging to the village can be seen emerging from the water.

Considering Haweswater is in a remote setting and is not one of the best known of the lakes, it is surprising how many cars arrive here at the weekend, filling the car park and lining the edges of the road. More often than not the cars are empty, the owners of which are up on the high fells, most notably High Street, the crowning peak. Wainwright spent two years walking these fells and in all that time he met no-one. That was in the mid-fifties, when the villagers were being evicted, but even today it is possible to spend a whole day walking here and not encounter anyone.

◆ Return the same way along the road, taking the first right turning in the trees at the end of the reservoir, which crosses over a bridge.

The road rises quite steeply, wooded on the right, with views towards Bampton on the left. It soon arrives at an area of high moorland with gorse bushes and marram grass, a complete contrast to the lush green valley of the River Lowther below.

◆ The road comes to an open crossroads. Turn left, signed for 'Bampton', along a single track road winding down to a T-junction. Turn left and continue between farm buildings, towards the church tower at Bampton Grange. Turn right at the T-junction, crossing over the bridge and heading towards the church.

Bampton Grange is the sister village of Bampton, half a mile away. As with most of the villages in this part of the district it is a sleepy and attractive place, set on the River Lowther, overlooked by the church of Saint Patrick which stands just after the bridge. The inn, at the centre of the village on the left, is called The Crown and Mitre and has its front door framed by stone columns.

✦ Take the first left after the village, signed for 'Knipe and Whale'.

The single track road leads slightly uphill to another area of open moorland, passing on the right a rocky topped fell, Knipe Scar: more evidence of the limestone in the region. There are views to the left over the farmland of the Lowther Valley.

✦ At the telephone box turn right through the gate and follow the road as it winds up to a second gate. Continue ahead towards Askham.

The road climbs for a short way after the gates before levelling and eventually heading downhill and passing a lane on the right leading to Whale, a cluster of estate cottages where workers at Lowther Park would have lived.

✦ Cross the river and continue to the junction. Bear right, back into Askham. Continue through the houses and turn left a quarter of a mile after the village, towards Celleron. Keep left and follow the road back to the B5320. Turn left for Pooley Bridge (1 mile).

The Western Lakes

RAVENGLASS AND WASTWATER

FROM THE SEA TO LAKELAND'S DEEPEST LAKE

Starting point: Ravenglass station (SD085964)

Distance: 25 or 30 miles

Terrain: Quiet lanes, some optional off-road sections.

Maps: Unfortunately, this route straddles two of the OS Landranger maps: 89 and 96. The OS Lakes Touring Map (1 inch to the mile) has a mile or so missing from its western edge. The best option then is the OS Outdoor Leisure Map 6 which covers the whole route at the best possible scale.

Public Toilets: Ravenglass railway station, Eskdale Green.

Refreshments: Ravenglass: cafés on 'seafront' & at station. Muncaster Castle: tearoom; No shortage of village inns around the route.

Apart from an unavoidable few miles along the A595 (which is used as part of the route for the mammoth Cumbria Cycleway) this route sticks to quiet country lanes, hills are fairly continuous, but not very severe. There are several optional routes for mountain bikers, including a 3 mile stretch along the lower slopes of Muncaster Fell. Wastwater is the Lake District's deepest lake at 258 feet and with its screes running straight into the water it is the most dramatic. There is a road along one side only, so a trip to Wasdale Head (an extra 2.5 miles) means returning the same way. Wasdale is real walking country, the starting point for many paths into the high fells, such as Scafell, Kirk Fell and Great Gable.

✦ Start in the railway car park in Ravenglass.

Ravenglass is the start of the Ravenglass and Eskdale Railway (or 'La'al Ratty' as it is known locally) which crosses some very pleasant countryside, finishing near Boot in Eskdale. Unfortunately, it doesn't take bikes – it isn't big enough.

The quiet village overlooks the estuary of the River Esk, which cuts between sand dunes to join the Irish Sea. There is a small café on the 'seafront' and also 'The Ratty Arms' which stands next to the railway. There are footpaths along the edge of a stoney beach, but take care, as most of the sands are classed as danger areas.

✦ Turn right out of the station car park and follow the road out of the village.

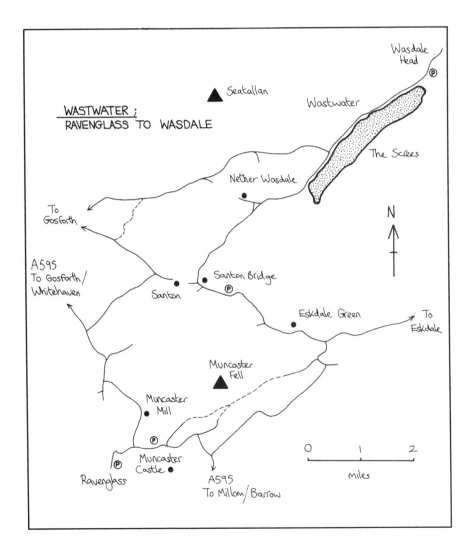

Look out for a footpath on the right immediately after the village which leads to Glannoventa, a Roman sea port, though all that remains are some walls that were once part of the bath house, now known as 'Walls Castle'. The path continues to Muncaster Castle, visited later on the route.

✦ At the T-junction with the A595 turn left, uphill, heading for Gosforth.

Muncaster Mill is situated to the right after $3/4$ mile, a late 18th century water-powered corn mill with waterwheel. Open daily, except Saturdays, throughout the season.

✦ Continue along the road another 2 miles through the village of Holmrook. Turn right after the village, signed 'Santon Bridge 2½ miles'. Follow the road between farmed fields and bear left at the T-junction, signed to Gosforth. Follow the road for just over 1 mile, then bear right along a farm trackway used as a bridleway. Cross the river via Hallbolton Bridge, shortly after which the path divides. Either route will suffice, leading in half a mile up to the road.

The road is a tree-lined lane leading downhill at first, then levelling out. On the left are gorse and ferns. On the right are views over fields and trees and the Wastwater screes.

✦ Turn left for Wasdale and climb to a cattle grid. The road crosses a grassy common and drops down to the lake.

Wastwater is renowned as the most haunting of the sixteen lakes. The famous screes slide straight into the clear water, and apparently continue right down to the bottom of the lake, 258 feet away. A totally unspoilt lake, with no boats to shatter the calm. Sheer and severe, just as Nature intended. However, it was under threat recently as plans were drawn up to deepen the lake and remove water for the nuclear plant at Sellafield, not too many miles away. In the end Wastwater was spared, and more water was withdrawn from Ennerdale Water.

✦ For Wasdale Head bear left and follow the road along the lake (3 miles). Return the same way.

Wasdale Head is caught between the highest fells in England. It is therefore the start of many of the Lake District's great walks, such as the ascent of Scafell. The famous Wasdale Head inn and hotel originally provided for the sheep drovers who had to travel through the mountains. Today it is the haunt of climbers, and many famous mountaineers have stayed here. A bridleway to the right leads to the minute church of Saint Olaf, over 400 years old, and reputed to be the smallest church in England.

Wastwater, looking towards Great Gable

✦ Return the same way along the lake road, but this time continue the entire length of the lake. Instead of bearing right, enter the trees close to the foot of the lake, passing Wasdale Hall youth hostel on the left. At the junction bear left, signed 'Santon Bridge 2 miles'. Turn left over the bridge, again signed 'Santon Bridge'. Follow the road through the trees, rising slightly, then dropping steadily (14%) into the village.

Santon Bridge is clustered around the bridge of its name, which crosses the River Irt. The Bridge Inn (across the bridge) is the home of the annual 'Biggest Liar in the World' competition. There is also a craft shop selling locally made wares.

✦ Bear left in Santon Bridge, heading for Eskdale Green (2 miles).

The road passes through a forested area. On the left is the Miterdale Forest, several miles of forest roads through mixed conifers which are open to cyclists. Also there is a car park and picnic site.

The road drops steeply into Eskdale Green, where you will find a couple of inns and two stations for the 'La'al Ratty' railway. After the second station on the right is a bridleway (relatively flat) leading across the lower section of Muncaster Fell along a forest trackway. Where the path forks after High Eskhole keep left if you want to remain on the low level route, though both paths eventually join the A595 near Muncaster Castle.

The left turning after Eskdale Green, opposite the King George IV pub leads along Eskdale, a very scenic road beside which runs the 'La'al Ratty' for 1.5 miles to its terminus at Dalegarth Station, where there is a café if you're desperate for sustenance. Also of interest close to the station is Eskdale Mill, another restored water-powered corn mill, open throughout the season, closed on Saturdays. The Eskdale road continues to the steep rise of the Hardnott Pass leading over to Dunnerdale and Little Langdale.

✦ Follow the road through Eskdale Green, taking the next right.

The narrow road passes through woodlands and plantations, with glimpses of the River Esk alongside on the right. There is a brief steep climb, then the road drops downhill, winding continually. Where the lane meets the main road there is a good view of Muncaster Castle to the right.

✦ Turn right onto the A595 and follow the road as it climbs steadily. There is a sharp left bend after which the gradient becomes more severe. Continue to the castle entrance on the left, in just under 1 mile.

Muncaster Castle was originally a pele tower built upon Roman remains. In the 1860s it was converted into the castle as it stands today: a fine Lakeland mansion. From the castle are the best views of Eskdale. The gardens, famed for their azaleas and rhododendrons, are best seen in spring, but are excellent in the autumn as well. Part of the grounds are used as an owl sanctuary, the birds being bred and then released into the wilds. There are toilets, tearoom and shop. Open daily throughout the season, except Monday.

✦ Continue along the road from the castle gates, dropping down into Ravenglass (1 mile). Bear left at the bottom for the village. The station car park is on the left.

Muncaster Castle

ENNERDALE WATER & ENNERDALE FOREST

A WEST SIDE STORY

Starting point: There is ample parking at the Bowness Knott car park, where there are toilets.

Distance/terrain/time: various.

Public toilets: see above.

Refreshments: refreshment vehicle in season at Bowness Knott. For further refreshment seek out Ennerdale Bridge, to the north-west of the lake.

Not a detailed circular route this time, as detailed route descriptions would be pointless. Once past the lake there is very little to see except trees. There is an extensive network of good tracks through the forest, which the Forestry Commission kindly allow cyclists to use, which can be followed in a variety of ways to make a circular route as far as Black Sail Hut Youth Hostel, returning along the opposite bank of the River Liza.

Ennerdale is difficult, but not impossible to reach without a car, the nearest railway station being in Whitehaven. Follow the A595 towards Egremont, but bear left along the B5295, through Cleator Moor, then follow the lanes along the River Ehen to Ennerdale Bridge.

Some people find being surrounded by dense trees quite oppressive, while others enjoy the isolation. There are views of the nearby fells from the higher ground, reached, unfortunately, along dead-end trackways.

Those with mountain bikes might like to make a circular route including Wastwater via the Black Sail Pass or Buttermere, Crummock Water and Loweswater via the Scarth Gap Pass. The Black Sail Pass is surprisingly flat on top and quite cycleable.

Ennerdale Water is the most westerly of the lakes and the most remote. It is the only one of the sixteen lakes without a road along at least one of its shores. It is 2.5 miles long and has for many years been used as a reservoir, supplying the west-coast towns, including the nuclear plant at Sellafield, the largest employer in the immediate area, which, sadly, is visible from many of the high fells in the vicinity.

In the late 1970s, there were proposals to increase the amount of water available from Ennerdale by raising the water level by several feet, which would have resulted in the loss of considerable amounts of the surrounding fields and forest, and would mean the building of embankments of up to 10 feet high. Thankfully there was a public outcry and, largely due to intervention of the National Trust, the plans were scrapped. Ennerdale was spared . . . but for how long?

Ennerdale Water

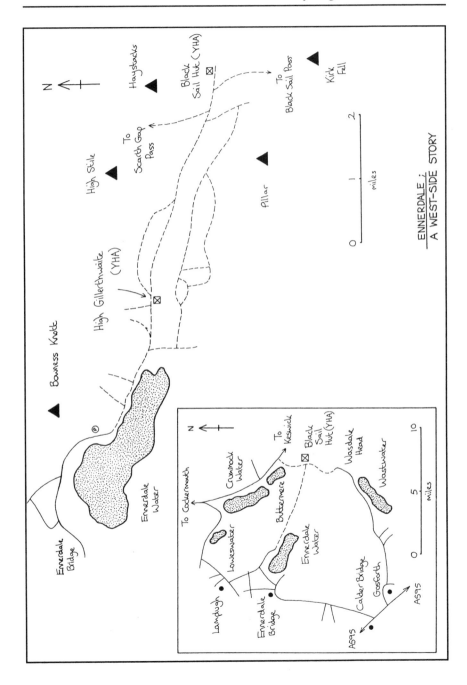

ENNERDALE :
A WEST-SIDE STORY

Coleridge was fond of Ennerdale. He first came with Wordsworth, while they toured the lakes together in 1799, and three years later he came alone, noting that the lake was 'fiddle-shaped', which it is, more or less. The valley was very different then, completely bare of its forest, as the Forestry Commission only came along and began planting in the 1920s, and was at first condemned by lovers of Ennerdale for 'ruining' the valley with straight rows of non-native trees. Today, the Forestry Commission strive to create softer landscapes by planting trees along the natural contours of the land, thinning trees out towards the top of a fell, rather than stopping the plantation in a severe and un-natural line, and they plant, as far as possible, a variety of different trees.

There are two Youth Hostels in Ennerdale. The first is Gillerthwaite, 1 mile after the end of the lake. The other is Black Sail Hut at the edge of the forest: a squat, stone building, once a shepherds' bothy, which still has only three rooms and no electricity. It stands completely alone, surrounded by high fells and fallen boulders, ten miles from the nearest settlement, with no access for motor vehicles, making it the most cut-off Youth Hostel in Lakeland, at the end of the loneliest valley.

LOWESWATER

THE FELLBARROW ROUND

Starting point: Loweswater: lay-by at Waterend, next to telephone box (NY118224).

Distance: 12 miles.

Terrain: Good roads, mainly very quiet lanes. Some fairly steep ascents on return journey.

Maps: OS Landranger 89; OS Outdoor Leisure 4; OS Lakes Touring Map.

Public Toilets: Sorry . . . None at all. You'll have to make use of pubs or hedges.

Refreshments: Low Lorton: pub; Loweswater: pub; cafés etc in Buttermere, 4 miles away.

✦ To Loweswater from the west coast: 10 miles north of Whitehaven on the A5086, bear right after Mockerkin Tarn, straight through the village of Mockerkin. Turn left at Fangs Brow and freewheel down the steep hill to the lake.

This short route around Fellbarrow is ideal to fill a couple of hours if you happen to be in the area. The roads are mainly flat, except for a climb between Mosser and Loweswater on the way back. The country-side is gentle pastures, not at all common for the Lake District. Well suited to those times when everywhere else is crawling with holiday-makers.

✦ From the car park at Loweswater head south-east along the lane towards Loweswater village (1³/₄ miles).

Loweswater means 'leafy lake', after the woodlands which cover its far shore, now owned by the National Trust. To the south-east there are views of the high fells, namely Mellbreak, Hen Comb and the giant of the area, Grasmoor. At Waterend there is a Camping Barn, part of a string that circle the Lake District, especially suited for the touring cyclist, as it eliminates the need to carry a weighty tent around with you. You take your own sleeping bag and so on, as you are basically hiring a roof over your head. It's warmer than sleeping under the stars.

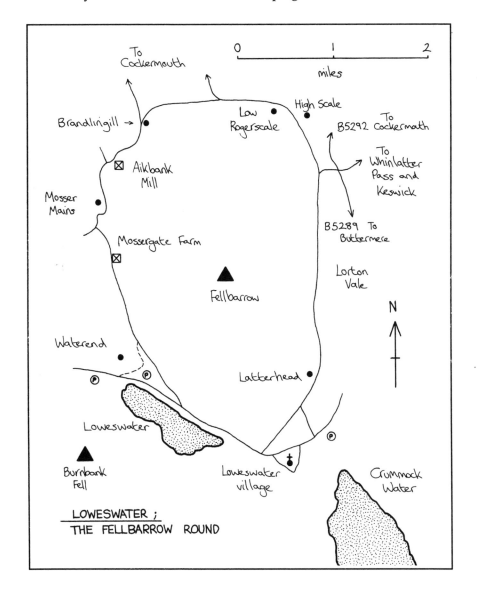

LOWESWATER ;
THE FELLBARROW ROUND

The road along the lake gives good views to the opposite woodlands and the backdrop fell, Carling Knott. For mountain bikers there is a bridleway running along the far shore, reached via a driveway in Waterend, involving quite a steep climb up to 'Hudson Place', after which it is quite flat. The track rejoins the road at the end of the lake.

Loweswater, looking east towards Grasmoor (right) and Whiteside

✦ Continue past the lake and bear left towards Thackthwaite.

For Loweswater village continue straight ahead after the lake and bear right. This was formerly the hamlet of Kirkstile, where you will find the Kirkstile Inn and the Church of Saint Bartholomew, built by the villagers in 1884 to replace an earlier building.

✦ Follow the road, slightly uphill, between farm buildings and through the hamlet of Thackthwaite.

To the right is the Vale of Lorton, an attractive, lush green valley, through which flows the River Cocker on its way to Cockermouth. 1.25 miles after Thackthwaite there is a right turning for Low Lorton. To make a detour here to its pub, cross the bridge and bear left at the crossroads.

✦ Follow the road around to the left, signed for 'Rogerscale 1 mile'.

The road leads slightly uphill and passes Low Rogerscale Farm on the left. On the right are views over the vale and the River Cocker towards Cockermouth in the north.

✦ Cross a small stone bridge over a stream and take the immediate left turning along Mirk Lane.

On the left are the numerous grassy hills that fall under the umbrella name of 'Fellbarrow', 416 metres at the summit and, in Wainwright's opinion, "pleasant, but unexciting". It is an unspoilt fell in a rural and peaceful area, and offers several miles of easy walking through sheep pastures and gives surprisingly good views from its summit.

✦ Turn left at the T-junction, through the hamlet of Brandlingill, after which the road climbs slightly. Pass Wood Farm on the right and Aikbank Mill on the left. Turn left at the junction, signed for 'Mosser ¹/₂ mile'. Follow the road through the hamlet of Mosser Mains, as it bears right and comes to an open grassy area. Turn left here along a narrow road leading uphill towards Fellbarrow.

According to Wainwright, Aikbank Mill (the mill itself now lending its name to a hamlet) is a "neat and colourful" cluster of buildings that "cries aloud to be put on canvas". In his 'Pictorial Guide to the Western Fells' (1966) he called for the artists of Cockermouth to "arise" and head there to paint it.

Mosser Mains is a quiet hamlet of brick, where all the woodwork: doors and window frames, seems to be painted a uniform red. This is a farming community and the road between its barns and buildings is likely to be muddy, so take care. To the left there is a public footpath out onto Fellbarrow via Fellside Farm.

✦ Continue past Mossergate Farm and High Mosser and begin the descent towards Loweswater. Just under a mile after High Mosser bear right along a bridleway which will bring you back to the lay-by at Waterend.

Appendices

Cycling Links between Towns

In many cases there are only main roads between towns, which means the cyclist has no choice but to take that route, unless, as in the case of Windermere and Ullswater, there are ferries which can make the journey so much safer and more pleasurable.

Kendal/Oxenholme to Windermere

The only railway that still exists travelling into the heart of the Lake District is the Windermere line, which begins at Oxenholme, 2 miles south of Kendal. There are many small lanes weaving their way towards Windermere and Bowness, but they are fairly steep. There are two main roads, the A591, by-passing Kendal and heading straight into Windermere, and the A5074 approaching Windermere and Bowness from the south. There is a much quieter B road which can be followed for much of the way into Bowness, the B5284, but probably the best way to reach Windermere is to stick to the train.

Windermere to Ambleside

The most obvious and direct route is via the A591 along the side of the lake, but this can be very busy and is quite narrow for the amount of traffic it has to carry. It can be avoided in the summer months by the lazy and very scenic route: dropping through Windermere to Bowness and taking the steam ferry to Waterhead, then riding the last mile. This is certainly worth doing at some point in your holiday anyway, especially for the views. Cycles travel for half the adult fare. You can check that the steamers are operating at the Tourist Information Centre in Windermere, close to the station.

The other way is again from Bowness. Continue heading south for half a mile after the steamer pier and bear right, following signs for the chain-ferry across the lake to Sawrey and Hawkhead. This ferry runs all year (weather permitting) and links the two shores. The charge for cyclists is minimal. If there is a line of cars waiting, cycle to the front and wait to be directed on board. Once the passage is underway there are good views up and down the lake.

Bowness-on-Windermere

Once on the opposite shore there is an initial uphill struggle, then it is relatively untaxing all the way. Follow the road through the villages of Far and Near Sawrey, past Esthwaite Water and through Hawkshead. A further 5 miles (through very pleasant countryside) will bring you to a T-junction after the River Brathay. Ambleside is 1 mile to the right.

Ambleside to Keswick

There are very few choices here but to take the busy A591 past Rydal Water and Grasmere, which then begins to climb slightly at Dunmail Raise (where a battle was fought and the body of King Dunmail is supposed to be buried beneath the mound of stones that now occupies the central reserve). It is worth taking the left turning directly before Thirlmere, which will take you on a pleasant trip along the west bank of the 3.5 mile reservoir. Towards the northern end of the lake there is a choice of direction. Either carry on straight ahead and bear left when you come to the main road (A591) which will lead you to Keswick (3 miles, dual carriageway part of the way).

Alternatively, for a more pleasant, but less direct route bear right at the head of Thirlmere and cross the afore-mentioned dam. Follow the lane past a camp site (on the right) to the main road. Bear right for half a mile then left along Saint John's in the Vale, following the course of Saint John's Beck. 3 miles after the main road bear left crossing the beck, and follow the road to the right. Keep left, following the signs for Castlerigg Stone Circle, which you will find in the middle of a walled field, with a parking lay-by on the right. There are 38 stones forming the Bronze Age circle.

Keep straight ahead after the stone circle and drop down into Keswick town centre.

Keswick to Cockermouth

Cockermouth is not actually in the Lake District, being just west of the boundary, but anyone interested in Wordsworth will want to visit his birthplace, now known as Wordsworth House, on the town's main street.

The most obvious route is via the A66, signed (conveniently) Cockermouth. This is a main road, a dual carriageway in parts and has little to offer the cyclist except perhaps exhaust fumes, and what could be a pleasant stretch along the western bank of Bassenthwaite Lake is ruined. Alternatively, the A591 heads around the opposite shore of Bassenthwaite. Turn left after the lake and follow the lanes through the villages of Embleton and Lambfoot into Cockermouth town centre.

The only other direct route is via the Whinlatter Pass. Follow the A66 Cockermouth road out of Keswick, and bear left to the village of Braithwaite, along the B5292. There is quite a steep climb at first through coniferous forests. There are good views to the right, northwards towards Bassenthwaite. There are various forest trails and picnic areas, as well as a Visitor Centre and café, where there is a walk-through replica of a badger sett, if you ever wondered what one was like inside. Drop down into the Lorton valley, through which flows the River Cocker (as in Cockermouth) and bear right. This road leads in 4 miles directly into the town centre.

Keswick to Penrith

Again, Penrith is not in the Lake District, but is mentioned here as it has a railway station, and is therefore important for those relying on the train to get them and their bikes to the northern lakes. The most direct route is by the A66 which runs directly to Penrith, but again it is a busy road, a dual carriageway for much of the way. However, there are slight detours which greatly reduce the amount of time spent on the A road and make for a much safer and more scenic ride. From the town centre follow the A5271 along the River Greta, following signs for Penrith. On the outskirts of the town bear left, uphill, along the A591, and take the first right, still uphill, to Castlerigg Stone Circle. Follow the road downhill and bear right at the T-junction at the bottom. Bear right again onto a larger road and follow it to the A66 (about 1 mile). Cross over the A66 and take the turning almost opposite, for Threlkeld. There is an inn here if you're ready for some refreshment. Follow the road through the village, past the church and back onto the A-road, continuing east. In two miles you will pass an inn and telephone box on the left, after which take the first right. Along this lane take the second right turning, AFTER the river. The road passes through the hamlet of Wallthwaite, then bends to the left, passing between open fields, crossing a dismantled railway then ending in a T-junction. Turn left, which brings you in a quarter of a mile back to the A66. Turn right. In another mile turn left, keeping parallel with the main road, joining in B5288 and bearing left to Greystoke. Pass through the village following the road east. From here Penrith is 4 miles. This road leads right into the town centre close to the railway station. A complicated route, and certainly less direct that the A66, but infinitely preferable.

Windermere to Penrith (and Ullswater)

From Windermere railway station, bear right for the A591, and turn left onto it, heading downhill signed for Ambleside. The road drops down steadily between large houses and expensive hotels and comes to a small roundabout. Take the last exit (i.e., bear right) onto the A592 for Ullswater and Penrith. The road rises gently between houses and then offers views to the left over Windermere and the central fells. Just under 1 mile from the roundabout on the right is Holehird Garden, described in some guidebooks as a "gardeners' garden", pride of the Lakeland Horticultural Society. Admission is free – yes, FREE – though donations are gratefully accepted. Beatrix Potter spent many summers at Holehird with her parents. The house was built in the mid-1800s and is now a Cheshire Home.

A mile after Holehird there are views down to the left over Troutbeck. After the Hayburn Inn on the left the road begins to wind, climbing steadily (16% in parts).

The Kirkstone Slate Quarry will come into view on the left, where the slate comes from for the Kirkstone Slate Gallery at Skelwith Bridge, eventually becoming everything from paving stones to coffee tables.

The road continues climbing to the Kirkstone Pass, where the aptly-named Kirkstone Pass Inn, a rather ramshackle looking building of white plastered stone, has the distinction of being the highest pub in Lakeland and one of the highest in the country. It was built in the 17th century, licensed in the 19th century and was originally called The Travellers Rest. From here the road drops very steeply, winding continually towards Brothers Water, an attractive, if somewhat angular lake, now owned by the National Trust. Legend has it that the name came from a tragedy centuries ago when two brothers drowned here, falling through the ice one winters day, though the name may simply be a corruption of its former title, Broad Water. Brothers Water was at one time considered to be the sixteenth lake, its place now being taken by Elterwater.

There are paths around most of the lake, making a pleasant circular walk of about an hour, passing through mixed woodland on the opposite shore, particularly picturesque in autumn.

The Brothers Water Inn stands on the main road on the left, behind which is a campsite and camping barn in the shelter of the high fells.

After the lake the road continues with no severe gradients. The next village is Patterdale: Saint Patrick's dale. According to legend the saint preached here and baptised from a well at the edge of Ullswater. A pleasant little village with an inn, hotel and youth hostel and not much else. Another mile down the road is Glenridding, the car park for Ullswater, from where the ferries leave, bound for Pooley Bridge at the opposite end of the lake. There are public toilets in the car park and towards the ferry pier.

The A592 continues along the length of Ullswater, undulating but without any steep climbs. 3.5 miles after the lake it joins the A66 at a large roundabout. Follow the signs at the second exit for Penrith town centre.

Brothers Water

Getting There by Train

Wordsworth was up in arms when he heard about proposals for the railway line extending to Windermere. "Is no nook of English ground secure from rash assault?"

Today, the Windermere line is the only rail route into the Lake District. Passengers from both north and south must change at Oxenholme, boarding the small train, usually full of rucksacks, that shuttles endlessly to Windermere and back. There is space for several cycles at the front and/or rear of the train, but be warned that BR's policy on transporting cycles varies by the week. For timetable details and current regulations, tel: 0539-720397.

For the Cumbrian west coast and western lakes a line runs from Preston to Barrow-in-Furness. For details tel: 0229-20805. From Barrow, a line continues along the coast and returns back inland to Carlisle. For details, tel: 0946-692414. Be warned, this train is only likely to stop at the various stations if requested to do so in advance.

British Rail now have a fixed charge for cycles on all Inter-City trains, and often reserve only enough space for two or three. To avoid disappointment, book your place at the station from which you intend to depart *several days in advance.* If, by any chance, your holiday is ruined by trains being unacceptably late or just not turning up at all, which does happen, then ask at any station for an address to write to with a written complaint, so that you can claim back some or all of your travel costs.

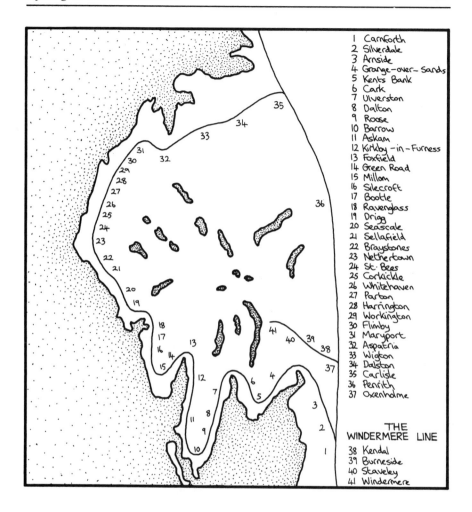

1 Carnforth
2 Silverdale
3 Arnside
4 Grange-over-Sands
5 Kents Bank
6 Cark
7 Ulverston
8 Dalton
9 Roose
10 Barrow
11 Askam
12 Kirkby-in-Furness
13 Foxfield
14 Green Road
15 Millom
16 Silecroft
17 Bootle
18 Ravenglass
19 Drigg
20 Seascale
21 Sellafield
22 Braystones
23 Nethertown
24 St. Bees
25 Corkickle
26 Whitehaven
27 Parton
28 Harrington
29 Workington
30 Flimby
31 Maryport
32 Aspatria
33 Wigton
34 Dalston
35 Carlisle
36 Penrith
37 Oxenholme

THE WINDERMERE LINE

38 Kendal
39 Burneside
40 Staveley
41 Windermere

RAILWAY STATIONS IN THE LAKE DISTRICT & CUMBRIA

Tourist Information Centres

The Lake District has some excellent Tourist Information Centres. Many have informative displays and exhibits and all have a wide range of leaflets and booklets on the various attractions and can book accommodation on request.

This is a list of some of the more relevant ones: any TIC. will be able to give you the numbers of others in the locality. Telephone numbers do change, so if you have trouble try Directory Enquiries who will supply any new number.

Ambleside
The Old Courthouse,
Church Street.
Tel: 0434-381696

Barrow-in-Furness
Civic Centre
Duke Street.
Tel: 0229-870156

Coniston
(Summer only)
16, Yewdale Road.
Tel: 05394-41533

Egremont
(For the Western Lakes)
12 Main St.
Tel: 0946-820693

Glenridding/Ullswater
(Summer only)
Main car park.
Tel: 07684-82414

Grasmere
(Summer only)
Red Bank Road,
Tel: 05394-35245

Keswick
Moot Hall,
Market Square.
Tel: 07687-72645

Windermere
Lowes Court Gallery,
Victoria Street.
05394-46499

Vegans/vegetarians And Wholefood Enthusiasts

If you fall into one of the above categories, you may be pleasantly surprised at how well the Lake District provides for you. Most restaurants now provide a vegetarian option (even if it's the standard vegetable chilli or lasagne) and vegans can usually get a jacket potato and salad if nothing else, but remember to take your own margarine.

Here is a town by town list of exclusively vegetarian/vegan restaurants and B&Bs.

AMBLESIDE
Zeffirelli's Wholefood Pizzeria and The Garden Room Cafe: Compston Road. Wholefood/vegetarian/vegan.
The Old Smithy (chippy): The Slack. Vegetarian/vegan menu.

CONISTON
Beech Tree Vegetarian Guesthouse: Yewdale Road. Meals available for non-residents. Booking essential.

GRASMERE
The Rowan Tree Restaurant: Langdale Road. Vegetarian/vegan.

HAWKSHEAD
Room With a View: above a gift shop in the centre of the village. Vegetarian, not so good for Vegans.

KENDAL
Waterside Wholefood Shop & Café: Kent View. Wholefood/vegetarian/vegan.

Crosthwaite Mill: Crosthwaite, Near Kendal. Vegetarian restaurant. Vegan by request. Booking essential.
Great Little Tea Shop: Lake Road. Vegetarian/vegan.
Orchard House Vegetarian Guesthouse: Borrowdale Road

PENRITH:

The Watermill Tearoom, Little Salkeld, Near Penrith.

In addition, most towns have at least one well-stocked health food shop which has available a selection of suitable take-away food: sandwiches, pies, pasties etc.

Further Reading

There are hundreds of books on the Lake District and dozens of Lakeland bookshops that sell them. These are just a few titles that I found indispensable.

❏ *Good Guide to the Lakes* by Hunter Davies (Pub: Forster Davies Ltd). The only guide you should need. A pocket-sized paperback, reasonably priced. Regularly updated. Information about every aspect of the Lake District.

❏ *A Walk Around the Lakes* by Hunter Davies, again. (Pub: Dent). Not so much a guide book as a literary journey. An insight into the people, places and practices of Lakeland.

❏ *The Thirlmere Way* by Tim Cappelli. (Pub: Sigma Press). Detailing a 130-mile walk from Thirlmere to Manchester, following a course as close to the underground aqueduct as possible.

❏ *The Pictorial Guides to the Lakeland Fells* by A. Wainwright (Pub: Michael Joseph). The fellwalkers' bibles: 7 volumes in all. See also the larger colour books such as *Fellwalking with Wainwright* and *Wainwright in the Valleys of Lakeland*.

*"Wainwright's Window" in Buttermere church, looking across the lake towards
Haystacks*

CYCLIST'S NOTEBOOK

Route	Date cycled	Comments

CYCLIST'S NOTEBOOK

Route	Date cycled	Comments

CYCLIST'S NOTEBOOK

Route	Date cycled	Comments

CYCLIST'S NOTEBOOK

Route	Date cycled	Comments

We have a wide selection of guides to individual towns, plus outdoor activities centred on walking and cycling in the great outdoors throughout England and Wales. This is a recent selection:

Cycling . . .

CYCLE UK! The essential guide to leisure cycling
– Les Lumsdon *(£9.95)*

OFF-BEAT CYCLING & MOUNTAIN BIKING IN THE PEAK DISTRICT
– Clive Smith *(£6.95)*

MORE OFF-BEAT CYCLING IN THE PEAK DISTRICT – Clive Smith *(£6.95)*

50 BEST CYCLE RIDES IN CHESHIRE – edited by Graham Beech *(£7.95)*

CYCLING IN THE COTSWOLDS – Stephen Hill *(£6.95)*

CYCLING IN THE CHILTERNS – Henry Tindell *(£7.95)*

CYCLING IN SOUTH WALES – Rosemary Evans *(£7.95)*

CYCLING IN LINCOLNSHIRE – Penny & Bill Howe *(£7.95)*

CYCLING IN NORTH STAFFORDSHIRE – Linda Wain *(£7.95)*

BY-WAY TRAVELS SOUTH OF LONDON – Geoff Marshall *(£7.95)*

Country Walking . . .

FIFTY CLASSIC WALKS IN THE PENNINES – Terry Marsh *(£7.95)*

RAMBLES IN NORTH WALES – Roger Redfern

HERITAGE WALKS IN THE PEAK DISTRICT – Clive Price

EAST CHESHIRE WALKS – Graham Beech

WEST CHESHIRE WALKS – Jen Darling

WEST PENNINE WALKS – Mike Cresswell

NEWARK AND SHERWOOD RAMBLES – Malcolm McKenzie *(£5.95)*

RAMBLES IN NORTH NOTTINGHAMSHIRE – Malcolm McKenzie

RAMBLES AROUND MANCHESTER – Mike Cresswell

WELSH WALKS: Dolgellau /Cambrian Coast – L. Main & M. Perrott *(£5.95)*

WELSH WALKS: Aberystwyth & District – L. Main & M. Perrott *(£5.95)*

– all of these books are currently £6.95 each, except where indicated